TO ALAN

WE WILL

THAN WE HAVE SEEN

BEFORE

GIVE YOURSELF PERMISSION

TO SEE + HEAR THE
WHISPER

The 1% Mindset:
The Stevie Kidd Pathway

STEVIEKIDD
PATHWAY

The 1% Mindset:
The Stevie Kidd Pathway

STEVIE KIDD

CONTENTS

FOREWORD

Before I start, I want to thank my family and friends for all the unconditional support that they give me every day. They understand that my life has to have a true meaning; to live by the principles of giving, serving and growing. Without them none of this would be possible. Their support has given me the content that's within this book, so for that I am entirely grateful. They are where I get my energy and the inspiration from.

There are many pinnacle moments captured in the chapters of this book. These are moments where even years later you remember them, and they always stay with you. They are fundamental messages from where you may have made life changes or shifted gear or direction. This happened to me when I met Dr Richard Bandler co-founder of NLP. The ripple effect he has created over the last 17 years has been truly remarkable. He has transformed my life, and I cannot publish this book without giving a huge thank you to him from the bottom of my heart.

I also have a role model in Lawrie Robertson who was my absolute compass in business and life. He was a dear customer and friend who I formed a unique friendship. Lawrie led his businesses right up to the age of 89 when he passed. It was a moment that had a deep impact on my life, but I adjusted, and I hear him every single day. In fact, now more than ever, his voice is a guiding light. I am blessed to have had you in my life Lawrie. For your teachings, lessons and support thank you very much,

Stevie x

INTRODUCTION
WHO ARE YOU?

'It's not what happens to you that defines your life, but how you react to it that matters.'

Epictetus

So, let's start by getting you to sit quietly and ask yourself these questions:

- Who are you?
- What do you want?
- How will you know that you have got what you want?
- Question to ask yourself right now?
- Are you happy?
- What IS happiness to you?
- Does knowing who you are create happiness?
- What do you now know about yourself?

So....

Let me take you to you the end of this book. Who you are, here at the start, will no longer exist. You can try and cheat, flick through to the end, skim it, but you'll still be here, back where you started. I'm Stevie Kidd and this is the book you never knew was for you. Until now.

My own journey through the twelve steps is here in black and white. A life lived in ten-year chunks, refined by reinvention. By reading every chapter and undertaking the exercises at the end of each chapter, you will rise to self-discover how far you can actually grow. Live your Pathway. Be in a position to understand how far you can take yourself with a 1% mindset. I'll be by your side.

Technical Terms

1% Mindset: On a piece of paper, you draw a line at the top of page with 2 arrows draw downwards, above the line you write "I live here" and under no circumstances are you dropping below those standards for anything or anyone….

Pinnacle Moment: I'm 12 years old - ahead of me are two lanes of a 400m running track. One lane is I run my lifeline and live my life how it's being conditioned for me to live. At the finishing line I die a miserable death.

or

I choose to run the other lane. In this lane, when I get to finishing line of death, I see myself sliding into my grave with a smile on my face saying, 'what an adventure!' It's like a Harrison ford movie. Star Wars or Raiders of the Lost Ark…

The Whisper: It is pure, and you really need to be still, very still and absolutely aligned to feel yourself being transported away from reality in an innovation bubble that's safe, warm and kind, then when you get to that point a soft voice appears pointing you to where to go and what to do… It's how everything has been designed in my life. The Stevie Kidd Pathway is another example of this.

If you do not condition yourself to practice alpha daydream state as often as you can, you will never master this state as this is where the real messages come from. New thinking new form of stillness creates a new reality.

To understand emotion, you can master emotion. I wrote down the emotion I experienced every hour, on the hour, for 8 years, from the ages of 8 to 16, as I knew if I understood emotion, I could master my emotions. The average person lives in 12 emotional states, we can experience over 27 emotional states.

Stevie Kidd

1

UNDERSTAND YOUR MIND

So, do you know who you are? Do understand you and your mind?

This is your book. Your tool to enable you to re-invent your identity and blueprint. You can write in it. Rip pages out and carry them around in your pocket. This book will be giving you the tools, the golden nuggets, the mystical moments that just capture you in a moment to simply enable you to turn up every day and attain the 1% mindset.

This first chapter, step one along the Stevie Kidd Pathway, contains stories about what my life demonstrates every 5 to 10 years. The 20 to 30 stories that will be told throughout this book, will inspire, motivate and stimulate your mind, but more critically they will demonstrate the importance of knowing your identity and living true to that identity.

In this book I will be demonstrating the major challenges I faced in my life and how knowing who I am meant I get up every single day and go again.

Now, I'll ask you:

If you had the mindset that no matter what gets in your way, you'll keep getting up, or go straight through, would this be a meaningful read?

Okay, first step on the Stevie Kidd Pathway. Understanding your mind. Tighten your laces, the going gets steep from the off. Strip away your education your business, your employment, answer this question, can you tell me who you are? Do you know who you are? Stay here for a few minutes and bathe yourself in that question, please.

What have you discovered right now in this moment?

So, let me give you a brief understanding of who I am. How I taught myself to understand my mind and take the first step on the pathway.

I was born in Paisley half a century ago and raised in Bridge of Weir. I always wanted to be an entrepreneur and my starting point was from the age of twelve. My role models were entrepreneurs and some family members. My first role models were Brian and Andy, who ran the local confectionary business and who I worked for selling confectionary from an ice cream van after school. They had a huge vision and they'd started as young as me. I got it into my mind that I wanted to be like them. They were relentless obsessives, they modelled it to me, and I mirrored them aggressively to a level of obsession, becoming an obsessive observer of all these types of people.

Life growing up wasn't all roses. There was an unpleasant incident in 1976, a one-off, that would be called abuse these days. I don't dwell on it, but it did lead me to yearn for ways to heal myself, to grow, in later years. The pinnacle moments of my youth formed the blueprint of the man. I discovered empathy when, on my newspaper round, one of the ladies that I was delivering to looked unhappy, so I asked, 'what's wrong?', she said she needed to get bread and milk, but was unable to leave the house. As she closed the door on me, I put down my newspaper bag and ran a mile to get her bread and milk from the shop. I was twelve years old. I remember coming back to the door and my mind saying pay attention to the response you get, it was like putting lights on a Christmas tree when she opened door, 'why would you do this?', she said. Already, I was obsessed with the feeling of making a difference, I responded, 'because I CAN'.

In that moment I made a rule and commitment, this will be my way of life, my whole life from this day forward. My uncle told me in later years that my Nan had said, 'there's something about that boy, something mystical. He is special'. It is another moment that stays with me each day.

Let's stop here for a moment and ask the following questions:

- Do you live inwardly or outwardly?
- Do you think of others more than think of yourself?
- How far are you willing to go to help others?

These are the three questions I used to align myself to other people from the age of 12. Though I didn't know it at the time, it is a strategy towards empathy.

Take a breath - what have you heard in your life that takes your breath away or gives you a moment? Remember and record that moment in this book. Reflect back on it as life will and is full of moments.

So, let's continue...

I felt very different about the frequency and energy I got from my nine jobs and the role models I mirrored there, to the frequency and energy I got from the classroom. To others it may have seemed bizarre, I know, but I paid attention to voices, pictures, movies that were created in my head about my future, when I was in school or when I was making money. The entrepreneurial world gave me a limitless timeline and potentiality, whereas education had both a limited timeline and limited potentiality mapped out in front of me. Choosing the entrepreneurial timeline meant it was easy to see where I had to go, along the path that lead to life being an adventure.

I remember my headmaster bumping into me in the street outside school one day and saying, 'Stevie, you need to get back into school.' and me saying to the headmaster, 'do you know who you are, sir, if I take the title of headmaster away?'. He glared at me very confused, and in that moment I just as if I was seeing through him. I saw somebody across the road. 'What are you looking at, Stevie?' I told him that I was looking at my twin who was five years ahead of me and already didn't need school. 'He is showing me the way sir', I told him. The twin is constantly with me all the time, he just keeps quantum jumping in 5-to-10-year timelines, I have come to understand that I will never catch him until the end of my life, which is fine, but remember we have much still to do and achieve.

This is a powerful visualisation technique and why should it not be? As we grow up as children, we constantly use our imagination, we dress up and play out our superheroes, so there's difference here.

It's fair to say education wasn't for me. I was captivated by stories, though. Always have been. Their power to immerse us, empower us to make that leap of imagination. I was paying attention to how I felt at that point forwards. I was aware of how I felt. My right brain, not just the left brain.

I decided that the world was my oyster, it's a Walt Disney movie of my making.

When I was seven years old, a young boy who would have been about five, Christopher Matthews died of leukaemia. It made me understand my mind on death in an instant. How long have I got, I thought?

How long have you got? That was the question I posed to myself at this age? I knew in this moment life is for living.

One of the first stories I remember being enchanted by was the black and white 1957 film, 'Scrooge', that I watched when I was eight years old, cross-legged and open mouthed in front of the television, I was in this movie like I'd escaped into the TV set. The concept of past, present and future was used by Dickens to great dramatic effect in bringing about Scrooge's character transformation. The scene that stayed with me to this day is the haunting moment when Scrooge is taken to see his own grave by the Ghost of Christmas Future. That sent shivers down my spine and got me thinking about what I'd want my life to be. Existential stuff for an eight-year-old, I was a mystic-minor, remember. Mum had always looked after people, nurtured them, and I learned that empathy from her. Remember the milk and bread? It was one of the greatest gifts of my upbringing. One day I asked my mum why she helped people, her response was simply, 'because I can'. It's a moment that formed me and something I think about every single day.

Work, I was working up to. First the nine jobs by twelve, a work ethic modelled by my father, who I watched worked day and night. Then, I set my sights on leaving school and getting a job at the local leather factory. I went every day to ask if there was work going, forty-two days in a row. I had 3 companies I visited every day asking for work, my dad said, you're persistent I'll give you that, but he knew what I was like. Dad had watched me in my childhood, being relentless with my work ethic. That's the plan, I said, grinning. I wanted to keep the movie alive, amplify the movie in my head. I was relentless and obsessive, mirroring my role models in the confectionery business, Brian and Andy.

The manager finally took me on, mostly to stop me asking. I'd embedded my command. He handed me a broom and told me that I'd be shaving hide by twenty-one if I was good and I was lucky. I told him I'd be shaving hide a lot quicker than that and that I'd be leaving in nine months, the moment I'd saved the money to start being an entrepreneur. I was going to buy an ice cream van and confectionery van business from Brian and Andy and strike out on my own. The look of disbelief on his face.

I met an angel at the leather factory. His name was Willy Macmillan, and he was the oldest shaver in the factory. He was a hard worker all his life and set me a lot of good values. Willy said to me that I could do better than shaving leather and empowered me to believe in the dream. He was the one guy who would listen to my stories in what I wanted to do with my life, and he listened and gave great advice. I was raised to kneel to elders with utmost respect. It is a trait that has served me well. Willy was my angel.

In the beginning the game was we flip 400 hides a day my challenge was ask as many questions as I can in a day, it turned out to be a question a hide, so point is how many questions do you ask each day?

I became what I said I would be within a matter of months and was the youngest leather shaver the factory had ever seen. I felt protected there. From the smirking manager, from the argy-bargy of the rest of the older men. The day I left, when I'd saved enough to buy the business, as I said I would, they called me Willy's boy. I never saw Willy again and I will never forget him. I heard some years later that he'd passed, and I said a prayer for him and thanked him for being one of my angels. You have to take these moments to reflect on the lessons and the magic moments these people bring to your life

I cannot let you move on yet. please take a moment to be silent and think of the people that have passed that gave you value, morals and lessons... take a real three minutes of silence to let it come through.

Now we continue... what are you discovering so far?

I bought a confectionery business from Brian and Andy and got a patch on a scheme in Paisley. In this moment my frequency and purpose for life is off the scale, age and time does not even exist, it's a life of purpose now. I had this dream from the age of 12 and now it is reality. The business was fourteen thousand pounds, which I'd saved by working like crazy at the leather factory. It included the van, opening stock and the patch. It was a pinnacle moment for me. A moment I took to fly across my timeline to see all that I had done from above.

At first, I realised that this was very different to the after-school ice cream selling that I'd been doing for an hourly wage. It was 6am to midnight. I was worried that I couldn't hack it. I took two fifty-pence pieces from the float, locked the van and set off for the phone box on the corner. I rang Brian and said, look, this isn't what I signed up for. I'm just a seventeen-year-old boy. Brian said, this has you all over it, and hung up. I held the remaining 50p in my hand. I'd decide my future on the flip of a coin. Just before I span the coin, a lady shouted, 'you'll last 3 months. All the rest never passed 3 months, too rough a scheme for them', so I've this thought ringing in my ears. In a flash, I said out loud, 'heads I get my money back from Brian, which he'd promised when I'd handed it over. Tails, I carry on'.

Well… three stops later on the round, I met my wife, Lesley. We would get together years later. By landing heads, I not only met my wife, but I also learned what working among the truly disadvantaged was like. Parts of the scheme were tough. While I was handing out the '99s, I listened to people's stories and honed my skills. I thought, how do I understand your mind? It was good for business and good for the community. I honed the skill of mastering and understanding your mind while selling to those people. I learnt how to understand them all by paying attention. It took love, unconditional love. I was working at the highest frequency. My fuel of choice was trust and respect. I could leverage a five hundred to one thousand people a day.

Now at this point ask yourself, do you understand YOU?

You will not understand others if you cannot understand yourself! So, the question at the start of this book was "do you know who you are"?

The Stevie Kidd pathway is a life journey from me to a place where you do self-discover who you are and that leads you to new paths. I sold that business and went to work for a cash delivery firm. I was hanging about at home, with money in the bank, but nothing to do and my dad said, why don't you get a job where I work. So, I did. I'm back with a broom in my hand, sweeping the yard.

How would you feel at this point if this was you, starting all over again?

2 years later, I'm on my way to running the business for seven years. That's where my business education accelerated. I was barely twenty-three and I was running three depots for that firm. I was paying attention to people, and I started to build up a pattern. I went from a broom to a van, where it's just you and a steering wheel, to steering the whole company. A few years later, I was managing 200 people.

Another Brian was a mentor I looked up to and mirrored. His name was Brian Clark, and he played a huge part in my cash services journey. Brian told me that I was unaware that the day I left the business nobody would come close to my standards. I'd mirrored and modelled Brian and, lo and behold, he told me that my standards were higher than his. Now, this was because of role models that I was obsessed with and mirroring people who were getting the outcomes that I wanted to achieve. It's a fast-track path to success.

How did I do it?

I turned up. Every day. I had a vision and I had goals. I didn't know if this would be my last day on planet earth. I understood my mind. You see I was one for enjoying the present but always creating a greater future and environment in my mind, so just like a Disney movie, I would escape and constantly create future movies of my future life. That is the future of reinvention.

I'd served my apprenticeship by the age of 33 and was ready to strike out in the cash delivery business on my own. I'd done it because of a dispute with the firm I worked for. They wouldn't invest in the fleet. I insisted they did it for safety reasons. I was dismissed. I had no money. My dad lent me seventeen hundred quid to buy my first van. Again, I'd set up my own firm.

I am back at a starting line, having to start from the beginning again. How would you feel if this was you? What is it I am doing to consistently go again?

I had a vision to challenge the cash delivery business. We won and operated large contracts with FedEx and Alliance Boots. The firm, KDS Group, grew, with a few million-pound turnover, large workforce and fleet of vehicles. This experience led me into people development via the UK government-backed innovation projects and from that into personal coaching and beyond to the Stevie Kidd Pathway. My life has led me to the Stevie Kidd Pathway, it's brought me right to this point. This point here. This is where I am meant to be.

I quickly realised that a ten-year pathway could be built up. I learnt this from the ten-year pathways in my own life. You will read, as you take the pathway, and learn to understand how I got to where I am, while taking the journey yourself.

I've always been obsessed with people's states and stories, and I feel exactly the same way about yours.

Ask yourself, who are your role models? Have a good think because you're going to need them on this twelve-chapter pathway to transformation. Mine are my parents and grandparent, as you've read. The two Brian's. Willy, of course. Sir Alex Ferguson and Muhammad Ali. A dear friend and customer, Lawrie Robertson, who taught me to realise my goals and punch above my weight. Dr Richard Bandler, co-founder of NLP and the entrepreneurs who've been in my life journey to date. You will read other people who have had an impact on me throughout this book.

How can I get you to really engage with *you*? The world is in the outside not the inside, but we need to awaken the inside with a shock to realise we will take the outside by storm.

Clear your mind please... be still... are you ready?

Let's begin as we open the door to exercise one. As you walk through the door... the soft mat is on the floor on front of you. Walk through the door and lie on the mat. We will now do the exercise...

Exercise One: 'Scrooge Story'

I want you to go into a quiet state and give yourself permission to float to the end.

Lie down or sit with your eyes closed in your comfortable spot and imagine that you are at that moment we all have to face… the end of your life.

What is the story you attach to your life in this moment of stark realisation? Now just glance to the other screen as that's the next choice, this screen shows you what you will do, how far you will go, what your potential actually is, you can see, hear and feel clearly what's holding you back.

So now you have the stories you'd tell yourself at that moment, bring yourself back to the present knowing exactly what needs to be done from this point forward.

Take your time, enjoy the fact that you are still well and truly alive.

Now think about the meaning you attach to your life and come to the present. After arriving, you need to answer these two pinnacle questions:

Do you now realise you can do more and be more?

Do you now realise what's stopping you?

You, the new you. The one with the 1% mindset. What are you going to do now?

Write down, in the space below, or on a piece of paper you can leave in your special place, mine's the fridge door, ONE commitment you will make to each of the areas of your life. Starting from NOW. Then write down and cross out one thing that you will NO longer tolerate in each area of your life.

End of Exercise

My life is full of big stories, I don't have one, I have many. Are you in my world yet? That's where the magic lies. I'm stronger, wiser, more mature and, yet, still free. Why? Because I can demonstrate I know who I am, and I know where I am heading. My interpretation of life is that it's a journey and an adventure, as manifested in the Stevie Kidd Pathway. The more you know yourself, the bigger the adventure. I'll see you at the end of the book. To end, ask yourself:

- What are you going to do now?
- All I want you to ask yourself is:
- Could you be more and do more?
- What would you do here?
- Enjoy the rest of the book.

China Marathon Finishing Line

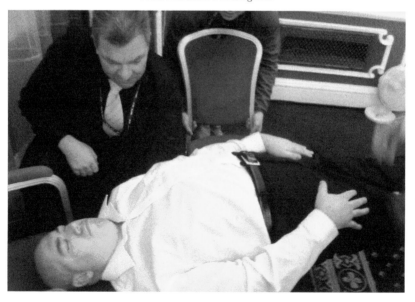

Personal Development under Dr. Richard Bandler, The Co-Founder of NLP

Stevie Kidd Climbing Mount Kilimanjaro in 2016

Stevie Kidd CEO of KDS Group

Stevie Kidd's Role Model and Mentor Lawrie Robertson

Stevie with Son Ryan at 3 Months

Stevie and Lesley Kidd

2

UNDERSTAND YOUR SUBCONSCIOUS

Time to understand your subconscious:

- How are you programmed?
- Do you just exist?
- Does your job or Business create your identity?
- Do you want to feel FREEDOM?

Understanding your subconscious

What's been installed in your younger years that leads you to believing that's the world you have to live in?

Ask yourself these questions:

- Who are you when you never ever give up?
- Who are you when you are relentless?
- Who are you when you doubt yourself?
- Are you aware of what holds you back?

- Do you think, or do you remember the majority of the time?
- Do your Beliefs get you the outcomes you want?
- How often do you challenge your beliefs... when you remember you are living in the past or when you think you are creating and designing your future in your mind?
- How do you spend the moments of your day?
- If we could take away everything you keep playing in your head that serves you no purpose, what would you do with that time when you get it back?

Remembering causes hesitation - You delay yourself or continue to trap yourself in a way that leads to not taking action. So, in the end you remain stuck.

Thinking creates action - It excites you, especially when with no critic or opinion, you time travel and innovate and design.

What I've found is... "If your heart is empty, you will not be able to run the 1% Mindset programme in your mind." Stevie Kidd

When we are connected, we thrive and believe anything is possible.

Some more questions towards understanding your subconscious:

- Where do you live in your head: "past", "present", or "future" - What gets all of your attention?
- How do you feel most days?
- Out of a score of 10, 10 being truly amazing, where do you live emotionally?
- What is your focus and direction?
- Are you aiming and setting targets in the right direction?
- Is something holding you back?
- Is it your mind, or the movie you play in your mind from a past experience that locks you into multiple future projections?
- What stops you from Being excited about your life?
- How much time have you lost each day playing the same programme every day?
- When you look at your life wheel and you see where you are right now and then look up and see how far you have to go to reach your goal, the question is: what beliefs stop you from taking action to move forward?

1% Mindset

Since the age of 12 I have immersed myself in the ability to design and create in 5-10-year chunks relating to my life. These chunks are rock solid and no matter what life throws at you will never fall below this line. You must remain focused on the end you have in mind all the time. Your role models set the bar, the line if you like. Modelling role models myself, kept me away from my own beliefs as they got the results I desired, so the objective was always, what's beyond this level of a world? For you to attain a new world beyond the level of world you are currently in means new thinking is required to create new realities.

I remember a Scottish minister in a private meeting with me, at the Scottish government building, saying to me, you are who you are because of your life and business experiences. It was true, I have had many life and business experience and have witnessed other people having many of their own life and business experience. When you've supported people for a living for most of your life, the mind you have is immersed in all walks of life. This means that you see a lot, especially when you are moving down the alley of life like a ten-pin bowling ball heading for a strike. The one thing you learn, is that just like the pins, you simply keep getting back up.

Pinnacle Moments Teacher Story:

When I was a young man, between the ages of twelve to sixteen, I was aware of powerful, forceful voices coming towards me. One directly at my head and one to the right-hand side.

At this point in my life, I'm in a daydream, if you like. I was able to work out true inspiration every time. Every time I set up a business or set about growing the company that I owned at the time, I went quiet. Through going quiet, I was able to raise those guiding voices that were in my head.

There were two teachers, in particular, in high school that were constantly telling me, 'You won't be able to do that' and 'get your head out of the clouds'.

'You Won't Be Able to Do That.'

'Get Your Head Out of The Clouds.'

The meaning of harnessing the subconscious mind is that the whisper was telling me to pay attention to the voices in my head, not the voices of those two teachers. That's why, rather than thinking about being pulled back, you won't be able to do that, get your head out of the clouds, Stevie, when I was thinking about what to do at the age of seventeen, I quickly realised something profound. If I paid attention to my mind and those two voices, rather than the negative voices of the two teachers, I could decide to switch the voices of the teachers' off. I realised that in switching them off, I'd replace the voices with the voices of two role models. Then I changed it to Muhammad Ali's mantra, 'I am the Greatest', how he uses language to manifest positive outcomes.

It's a simple story.

Me, being aware of what had been installed in my mind and the fact that those two negative mantras, 'you won't be able to do that' and 'get your head out of the clouds', were holding me back. They were locked in my subconscious and when I was on autopilot, I was believing it at a subconscious level. When I mastered communication between my subconscious and conscious mind, I became aware.

That is when you can take action and change your belief. That's what I did at that age. How many people go through their lives unaware of this? They see their business as a niggle... thinking, what's holding me back. They stay locked in that idea with their heads in the clouds and there is no change. Ever. I saw that that phrase was holding me back and I said, 'no chance' and replaced it with 'I am the greatest'.

My Learning Obsession

There was once a guy who enrolled on a Life Diploma course and the person running it was going on and on about Dr Richard Bandler, the co-founder of NLP. This guy did the first day. The person running the course was relentless about the other guy going to see Dr Bandler. The guy who'd done the open day, took the information, encased in a plain white envelope, took it home and, for want of anywhere better to put it, stuck it on the top of his fridge. The envelope laid there, like a loaded gun, until a gust of wind from the garden did its thing, eighteen months later. The guy on the open day was me, Stevie Kidd, the plain white envelope was just a plain white envelope. What was inside it was anything but plain. Anything but.

Eighteen months later, when that wind of change blew in from the garden because somebody had left the kitchen door open, and I was on the point of investing in a company, but having doubts, because I'd been told I couldn't be who I wanted to be, the gust of wind picked up the plain white envelope containing the explosive information and moved it to the front edge of the fridge. We'll call the wind, which was a whisper, after all, the wind of change. Then, that night, I awoke at 03:02 and went downstairs to the kitchen. I looked up at the fridge. Once my head went quiet and I looked up and saw an envelope on top of the fridge. The Whisper was pure, and I felt like I was being guided by a compass. I went to grab it and it fell on the floor and the flyer inside it fell out and the next thing that happened was that everything changed chemically, right across my neurology. Now, all of a sudden, I was signposted to go and see the man who'd co-founded NLP. It was a major moment in my life but happened in a very short and dynamic way. When you receive messages and you don't hear them, you may be missing out on the most major thing that could happen to you in your lifetime. If you remain conditioned in what you believe, you may miss out. So, all of a sudden, eighteen months after I was handed the plain white envelope, the flyer falls out of the envelope as I grab it and I take action immediately.

Within a week, I was sitting in a five-star hotel, ready to do the most expensive course I've ever done. This event is called Personal Enhancement. Twenty thousand pounds investment for three days with Dr Richard Bandler, just ten people in the room. It is all about understanding the mind and the brain.

A Question:

- Can you remember a time in your life when you were given a message, but you never acted on it?

Spend the next five minutes asking yourself these questions:

- When did I act on it?
- How long did it take me to act on it?
- Now that you've become aware how long it took you to act on it, ask yourself this,
- What stopped me from acting on it the first time I was given the message?

Dr Bandler

I became obsessed, relentlessly with everything that Dr Bandler had ever written or said or produced. What Dr Bandler was teaching me was everything about the conscious, unconscious and subconscious mind; everything about my Neurology. He was getting me to understand every aspect of Neurolinguistic Programming and neurology. Over a period of over ten years, I then invested heavily in going to America, all across the UK and over that length of time I purchased everything that man ever produced, ever wrote, all media and being on site, training with him. In short, he'd be my specialist subject on Mastermind. I even asked him at one time to become my coach. That in itself is a story, because the relentlessness of being coached by somebody at that level didn't faze me at all. He couldn't do it because the smallest group he works with is groups of ten. My concept, in my subconscious mind was to destroy who I was, to become who I am. The whole credit on this chapter, understanding your subconscious, has to go to Dr Richard Bandler. It is also about how I pre-frame myself by turning up and taking what I do very seriously. This was because I was always realising what I was learning was going to constantly reinvent and evolve who Stevie Kidd was. That's where the toolkit came from, *The Stevie Kidd Pathway*.

The Stevie Kidd Pathway

It has taken since 2007 for the Stevie Kidd Pathway to be fully formed, when I started doing events that were modelled on the teachings of the people that I was being developed by. These people include Tony Robbins, Dr Joe Dispenza, Professor Lipton, John La Valle and Dr Richard Bandler, of course.

I asked myself, what would lay beyond that? What led beyond that was, the subconscious mind, realising and understanding my neurology empowered me to know how to use it. This led me to then challenge the belief, which then led me, even in failure, doing multiple events in London and Scotland where naebody turned up. Naebody. This led to a Windsor Castle event, in St George's House, which was an event for twenty people. I went from naebody to everybody. All of them turned up.

Taking the business experience and the events experience and all of the development that I did, this combination led me to the Stevie Kidd Pathway. The Stevie Kidd Pathway was about an event that was about challenging and taking the theory and putting it into the practical sense. This is why the whole Pathway is a minimum two-year program, along which you will be constantly evolving, constantly being developed, where you seek to close the gaps between where you are to where you want to get to.

Then, the Pathway takes you to the science of understanding what truly goes on within you with introducing brain mapping. Then, we are introducing a series of events over the two years.

The first is Reach Your Peak Scotland. A hundred-hour program, over five days, undertaken over six months while you are in coaching.

Then we move on to Reach Your Peak Kilimanjaro.

Then, in the second year, taking you on to Reach Your Peak Everest Base Camp.

You will be asking yourself:

- How far can I go in constantly evolving and reaching my absolute potential?

The Stevie Kidd Pathway was about challenging my beliefs, but also it is about challenging your beliefs and the beliefs of everybody in terms of what one thinks an event should be and how you take somebody from something and turn them into who they were born to be, by constantly stripping away the beliefs that have been installed in them over a number of years.

That is what the Stevie Kidd Pathway is.

www.steviekidd.com

Exercise Two

Starting today, I will live my life without limits!

Today I am committing to one huge, unbelievable goal which is:

- My three smaller intentions which will take me closer to these intentions are:

    1.

    2.

    3.

Email the team at inspire@steviekidd.co.uk and hold yourself well and truly accountable. Send a video, an email, but outline what you plan to do to move yourself away from who you are, to live a life of absolute fulfilled potential. Worst outcome of this is that you do nothing. The best outcome of this is that you do something and take your first steps along the Pathway.

Everest Marathon 2017

The London Event Where Nobody Turned Up

Stevie Kidd Windsor Castle Leadership Event

Stevie Kidd with MindSpa

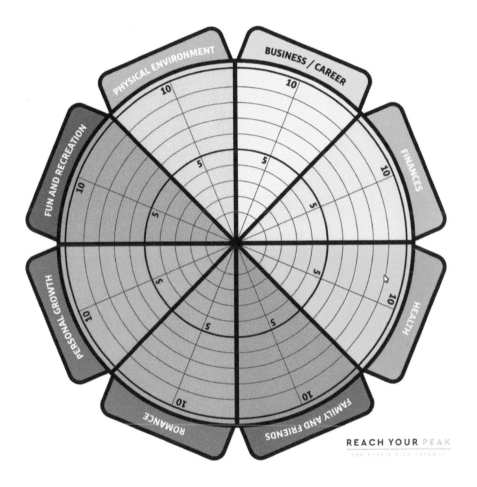

Wheel of Life Tool

Stevie and Ryan Creation of Reach Your Peak Scotland

"Stevie Kidd is the real deal when living the dream and achieving the impossible. He is a highly motivational guy who, with his passion, can and will enhance your life by motivating you to achieve your goals and to become better in your own endeavours."

Dr Richard Bandler: American author on modern psychological techniques and co-inventor of the internationally renowned Neuro-linguistic programming (NLP)

Stevie and Dr. Richard Bandler, Co-Founder of NLP

3

CHALLENGING REALITY

I would like to start this chapter by paying tribute to the genius of a man that is Dr Richard Bandler. Dr Bandler said to me, 'Stevie, opportunities are everywhere. Challenge them all. See them all. Hear them all. Feel them all.'

This book is twelve chapters; twelve steps, but it is also about awakening you to realising what lies within you. Pay attention to what you are seeing from an unconscious to a conscious level. Dr Bandler saw what was trapped, locked inside me and showed me a way of being able to pay attention and see and hear and listen. Dr Richard Bandler is a role model of mine.

The question is:

- Who are the role models who have given you messages?
- Give this question real consideration before answering.

- Who ARE the role models that gave you messages?
- Who are the people that are around you that put you in a different frequency?
- Who are the people that hold you accountable?
- Who are the people around you that inspire you?
- What messages have you acted upon that they gave you?

  or to put another way...

- What have you created in your head, just by being in their company, or hearing what they've said?
- On the flip side of the coin...
- What are the messages that you've not acted upon yet?
- Role models, who are they?

  Being around them, what happens to the stimulation in your mind, the voices and the feelings you have and the movies that you play in your head that you then act upon as a direct result of being around them.

- How many people have you met who are role models and you haven't acted on it?

Exercise Three

Give yourself permission to be silent, just for a moment. It's an exercise. Float back along your timeline. From above, see all the people in the past that you've had encounters with. People who have been exceptional for you in your life. Give yourself permission to drop down into the timeline and see, hear and feel what happened in those moments in your life. What was said to you? What was said to you at that time? What did you miss? What messages were you given that you didn't act upon? Reflect on the messages that you did act upon?

It is role models that have programmed me. It is role models that have programmed you. When you take the time to see, hear, feel, you will know.

- Now we come to the moment when we ask, why would I challenge reality?
- WHY would I want to challenge reality?
- Because I want to make a difference and be the difference.

I don't want to simply exist. I was born to have a legacy beyond my life. That is the meaning I give to my life. I'm here to make a contribution, I'm not here to simply exist.

I'm not here to simply exist.

Stop, and ask yourself, who are the role models that YOU

have been given and what voices did you choose to listen to when you were silent. Those voices will determine this. It's the whole purpose of meditation.

Mediation is where you access the whisper. It is within that whisper that the messages are that get you to challenge reality. Throughout this book you are hearing stories that are about challenging reality. This chapter has a master story about challenging reality and the story has a beginning, a middle and an end. It starts with a question:

- The question is a question about purpose. Do you know what your purpose is? It has a key bearing on how you challenge reality. So, I ask again, what is your purpose?
- Moving on from purpose, let me ask you something:
- How do you start your day?

How do you start your day, every day, and how does Stevie Kidd start his day and has done for decades now?

Stevie Kidd meditates. I'm in nature every single morning. From four in the morning until six in the morning. I'm there. I'm in nature, sitting on benches, becoming still. I'm practising alpha, meditating to stillness, meditating to nothing, then orchestrating the senses, one at a time, just like going to the gym. Just like building your muscles in a gym.

What is the number one part of your anatomy? The thing that drives you forward in everything that you do.

Your mind, your brain, your heart. So, how well do you look after it? I never miss a day. In fact, multiple times a day I condition my mind. Every opportunity, every day. Why, I hear you say? Simple, because you challenge reality you have to be in a creative and innovative state. So, we have to be in that state to be able to access it.

It is about ways you strip down the left side of the brain and open up the right side of the brain. You are accessing a brain frequency of gamma. Beyond gamma is epsilon, an out of body experience.

Imagine this: You drive, don't you? Now, do you remember the journey that you last took? Of course you don't. That's because you lose consciousness and go unconscious and it's your unconscious that goes onto autopilot. So, where do you go? When you start thinking and you go into this daydream and there's a stage beyond daydream state. Beyond that daydream state, you can challenge reality.

State is the number one thing. It is highly important to have the creativity and innovation to hear the messages, hear the whisper. My strategy of wanting to challenge reality is, 'how big can I think?' I've always believed I can challenge reality at such a level that it goes beyond the level it is at today. Every time, I think big. Think employability or distribution, my goal was to challenge reality and do something different, to capture truly global audiences. I've always believed that I can challenge reality at such a level that innovation is beyond a level that it's done in today's reality.

Or

You can create such an uproar that people say, no, that can't be done. This is why I've selected the following story as fitting for this chapter.

Why, I hear you say? Simple. To challenge reality, you have to be creative and innovative. That's the mindset you have to be in. You have to be in the residence of frequency that puts you into gamma. That's where you're able to challenge reality, when you are in this state of gamma, in that brain resonance. You have to be in that state to be able to do so. Practising meditation means it's very easy to go into that state. Am I saying, if you don't practice mediation, you'll find it hard to get into that state and hard to challenge innovation and creativity?

Yes.

What does challenging reality mean?

If you look at something that's 'in reality', that you admire, or something that you think is world-class. You have to ask yourself what's beyond that frequency? This can also be said for people. When I managed and supported, through coaching, a professional football manager, the biggest belief that he could see was to manage Rangers, but on my side, being the observer, I'm looking at him, seeing his potential and challenging his reality, to say, 'here's who I believe you can manage within five years of being in partnership with me'. As I opened my clenched fist, to reveal the note on the piece of paper I had concealed within my grip, it said 'Real Madrid'. It had been within my grip because I firmly believed it was within his. I was looking at where he was operating from. Was he operating from the left side of the brain, the right side of the brain, or both sides of the brain?

I wanted to know where his beliefs came from and why he wasn't challenging reality, in seeing what his opportunity was. Is Ronaldo challenging reality, being a footballer for multiple years? Playing for as long as he can, winning trophies in multiple countries. What's his next job? I put the idea to the manager that his ability to replicate that attitude was what he needed to do as a manager. So that they could go down as the greatest of all time, in football, player and management. Challenging reality.

Challenging Reality.
Rangers to Real Madrid.

The concept of being able to do that. How many years would somebody be able to replicate that? It comes down to Mohammed Ali, one of my role models from a young age, as you know. Watching what he told people he was going to do... be the greatest beyond his life... inspiring generations and generations to come. Challenging reality is what he did. By watching my own role models like Sir Alex Ferguson and Mohamed Ali, challenging reality beyond what people thought was possible, is why I am the way I am.

Like football, we need strategies to adopt the state of mind I am talking about. Before we talk about the pinnacle story, I'm going to help you with strategy, the strategies you need to be adopting each day, to access this state of mind, the one percent, so that you can challenge reality. I can only talk about my strategies. We've already spoken about the people you have to have around you, the unconditional love you have to have, the frequency you have to be on, all around you.

Another person I have around me is Sean Rose, a Reach Your Peak speaker whose story changed my life. Sean was paralysed in a skiing accident and was a speaker at my Windsor castle event 10 years ago and now is a frequent speaker on my Reach Your Peak Scotland event. This is a story about a time when I listened to ten ex-military stories and had to pick just one, at a college in Manchester, at an event for veterans who were being supported under the Walking the Wounded charity, to deliver a slot at my Windsor event. We then parted company and Sean was the first person I called, when I came to designing the Reach Your Peak event. We meet people not just for one thing, it can lead to deeper meanings. Sean has changed many entrepreneurs lives at events.

You need to practise gratefulness, gratitude. What are you grateful for every single day? At the start of the day, especially. Being in nature every day, we've spoken about, exercising the senses, doing them one at a time, but then bringing them all together... orchestrating them all. We now add four further fantastic strategies that bring this all together:

Music

For me, I'm not ashamed to say, that it's ABBA all the way for me. I can put ABBA on and leave and create something, it's the same with The Greatest Showman. I put that on and am swinging from the trapeze in seconds. It's the linguistics, the theme and the beat that takes you to a hypnotic trance. That's where you challenge. If you think of the Stevie Kidd Pathway, with the Greatest Showman, the Pathway is looking at amazing people like Tony Robbins, Professor Lipton, Dr Dispenza, Dr Bandler. I looked at how they were doing events, what their business model was. I'd play music and put myself into that state to ask myself what was beyond what they were doing? That is how the Windsor Castle event was designed. It was designed for me to deliver an event in the biggest castle in the world. I did it because all of the people I admired would take something like that on.

Music, obsession with fitness, obsession with humour and laughter…

Humour

Laughing often and with wild abandon release endorphins from the brain. It's important that this state happens because this is where juices are flowing. Laugh as often as you can, every single day. See the magic in EVERYTHING. If you struggle to recognise the magic, all you need to do is reframe it. Reframe it in a different meaning that gives you a new feeling. If you recognise that you don't see the magic in everything and you don't see the positive in everything. If you become where that you see things as negative, your unconscious will talk to your conscious mind. What you do to get into the positive way of living your life, is reframe and it with a different meaning what you recognise is that you're seeing things as negative, and you become aware of it. Your unconscious will talk to your conscious mind. Then, what you do to get into that way of living your life, reframe what needs to be reframed to give it a positive meaning. It's all about state, state, state.

It is massively important for you to be creative and innovative, if you can't get into that state and do all those things above you won't be able to get into that state and you won't be able to challenge reality.

Another strategy is to adopt and attain this state as a way of living. To do that, you get coached. The way to the state is to coach and be coached. Being coached not only means that you have to step up to a new frequency, why, because you are being held accountable. It means each day you have to deliver. If you're not being coached, then you are not being held accountable. Let's face it, if you're not being held accountable, you don't really bother, do you?

Being coached is a strategy for being able to achieve your potential. For you to challenge reality, you need to be operating at a peak state every day and to do that, you need to be coached. Being left to your own devices won't get the best out of you. You have to be solution minded. All the time. You can never complain and moan. You know what's coming next, don't you? Yes, that's right...

Exercise Four

You have to be solution-minded all of the time, to get into this state, so you can never complain, ever. Never moan, ever. It goes back to have positive people and environments in your life. I'm sitting in a corner office in a building and it's the biggest office in the building. The building is called, 'The Innovation Centre'. Wonder which state that puts me into?! At the same time, the office is floor to ceiling glass. It's a wow every day, for me and my clients. Environment has got a lot to do with it.

Start a day… pick a day… any day, but just pick one day, a day that's busy and then set about that day, but you're not allowed to moan or complain.

Think about that.

It doesn't matter if it's easy or difficult, because now you'll be able to see how far away from this frequency you need to be at, you are. I don't complain and moan any day. There's a difference between moaning and complaining and being passionate about wanting to get things right and trying to empower people round and about you to get people to the same level you are at. It is pulling people up to your frequency. You refuse to go DOWN to people's frequency. They have to come up to your frequency. There's a lot of work has to be done with you. As an individual, you have to be the example so that you bring people up.

You don't go down; you lift people up.

Think of the linguistics that you use. Power words. Mantras, affirmations. This is where Mohammed Ali punches his way into it. The internal dialogue of what you say inside and what you say outside, what you say out loud, is what keeps you in this state. Your physiology is such that you have to stand tall. You don't shrug your shoulders; you don't bow your head. You stand tall, as if the world was sucking your feet to the ground and the sun was pulling your head to the sky. Then you put in the dialogue and in that dialogue, there are POWER words.

This is not an act. It just becomes a way of life. An internal computer program that allows you and empowers you to be free and happy. I'm this state you believe you can do anything.

This next part is to do with your eyes. The eyes you look through, where you have to change the lens. Who are all the people you believe are geniuses in your life? You have to imagine you are looking through multiple sets of eyes. You have to imagine that, looking through these eyes you say, 'I truly am a genius'. I've got iron men, Dr Bandler, Lawrie Robertson, entrepreneur role models, Kenny Morrison, who swam the channel twice, multiple iron men, then, you've got Stevie Kidd on Everest base camp, China, Kilimanjaro, America. Those lenses go in. Ryan, my son and business partner, that lens goes in. Sir Alex Ferguson, my wife, Lesley, Corinne Hutton, Doug White. These are the lenses that I choose to look through.

You take your eyes out and you put everybody's else's eyes in. Look through their eyes and watch what happens. Dr Bandler once said to me, Stevie, you will know when you've made a change, when you look at something that you've looked at before in your mind and it has a NEW feeling. Change has occurred unconsciously.

THAT is how I measure my progress.

You have to be aware of the negative energy from people and environment and stay away. The objective every day is to be emotionally free. You have to be emotionally free to get into the state. Your past, you never visit it. That day is finished, the curtain is closed. Pay all of your attention to the front, I said PAY ALL YOUR ATTENTION to the front. Your eyes are at the front of your head, not the back. There's a reason for that.

When you go to bed at night, you do the rituals in the morning, but you supremely evaluate your day and you float up to the end and just before you close your eyes, you spin your hands round like a clock to the amount of hours you wish to sleep and when you close your eyes, you close the day off. You close that day off with a set of Velcro curtains and you look forward and you actually see yourself to the end of life. You actually see the journey that's ahead of you. You imagine all those things that you're going to grow into so that you can be greater than who you are today, tomorrow. Sometimes that great, that when you think about it, it becomes emotional. You close your eyes; you go to bed, and you wake up with no alarm clock. This is because your mind has been conditioned to wake you up. If you go to sleep for five hours, twenty-four minutes and twenty-three seconds, that's exactly when you wake up.

I've tested and proven that I can do that multiple times. You try it.

When you wake up, you go through the same ritual again on how you start your day. I start my day with an inventory, which is me scanning my body, scanning my body from head to toe. I'm connecting my mind, body and spirit. All of these things are hugely important for you to be able to get into a state where you are ready to receive the next story, which is about Kilimanjaro. What I have given you above is what I do every day to be able to challenge reality. I've given you the support exercises and the evidence of what you have to do to get to the stage that you are about to discover.

Fact: If you don't do the exercises, if you don't do the traits and strategies, that you've been given... you've got the evidence of what's taken Stevie Kidd to the places he's got to. Do the exercises and copy what I'm saying, yeh same things will happen to you because we all have the same neurology. It's how we use it that counts.

By challenging reality and asking myself, by checking in with my identity and asking myself, 'do I love myself, do

I like myself, do I know who I am'? If I'm being perfectly honest, the answer at that point in my life, when I started to challenge reality, was probably no. This is a very, VERY important point in this book. Even though I am challenging reality and sharing the exercises of how to go into this state of gamma or epsilon, an out of body experience, watching yourself, of whether it's a mystical moment, where you are creating innovation, the concept, and question is... can you do it when you don't even know who you are? No.

When you have a pinnacle moment a change can occur. Three pinnacle moments happened to me that brought about a change, leading me to be able to challenge reality.

The first was that I asked to go down and support a friend, Warren Hawke, who was doing a marathon. I was under the impression that the marathon was on land, but it wasn't, it was on water. In the water, up to your neck, if I'm going to be more precise. It was a hot, hot day, shafts of sunlight, dancing on water, dazzling the eyes of the expectant crowd. Hot day, time distorted, like something out of a Christopher Nolan movie. When it was over and the boat took me back to land, it took two and a half hours to make a twenty-minute trip. This was because I couldn't believe what I was seeing. I was seeing, for the first time with my own squinting eyes, somebody who was doing endurance swimming on a hot, hot day with a thick wet suit and swimming the length of Loch Lomond. The length of Loch Lomond. Forty kilometres. I couldn't comprehend it and I'd known Warren for many years.

The second pinnacle moment was when Warren signposted me to work with a manager. It was a manager of a professional football club. Stevie Kidd, coaching and supporting the manager of a football club, which led to him having a very successful season. When I first met him, his complete genius of insight, looking into a human being's soul, meant that he could see more potential in this manager, as an observer, than this gifted football club manager could see in himself. In that moment of first integration, Stevie challenged his reality by saying the biggest goal you'll have in your head is Rangers Football Club, trust the process, trust me and I'll take you to h-e-r-e. As he reveals who he is talking about, the football club manager goes into complete disbelief because he sees that it's Real Madrid that is that club. Humour and laughter was created, but even to this day, this football club manager will go to his grave remembering that very moment when Stevie Kidd challenged him by revealing that Real Madrid could be the alternative.

I challenged this football club manager's reality. He believed that Rangers was the biggest club he'd manage. I said I'd take him to Real Madrid in sixty months. This manager was locked in his own belief and his own story. Was Stevie Kidd the crazy one for conceiving of and believing in Real Madrid?! I'd been challenging his reality and it could only come about because I'd been challenging my own.

Driving back from Perth, ABBA on the car stereo, I asked myself what I was doing. I was challenging people, telling them to do great things, but what are you doing, Stevie? The voice and whisper kept going all the way home. Two hours. That's SOS to Fernando and back round again. I'm in a deep, deep state, and I'm asking myself, 'what are you doing?'

Pull over... Stop a minute.

I went home and what I did was, I wrote down the top ten things that would take me into the complete unknown and cause me extreme pain and discomfort that I wouldn't enjoy. That discomfort took me into action. I went for a run. It was horrible. Absolutely horrible. I did it because I wanted to destroy my identity and challenge reality. I wanted to create a new reality.

I wanted to cause real, real discomfort.

My question to you is:

- Where do you live? Do you live in comfort, or do you live in discomfort, and do you actually live in the unknown? Running is unknown to Stevie Kidd. China is unknown to Stevie Kidd, as you will learn, Kilimanjaro is unknown to Stevie Kidd... three unknowns.

Unknown is where you grow.

When I was on my way to Everest Base Camp, some years later and at five thousand metres, I realised that I was seeing the world on the outside very differently and at the same time was seeing my inner world very differently, too. What touched me greatly was the Sherpas that I climbed with. They were fascinated with my powerful head torch, that illuminated the way in the bitterly cold darkness. These guys had been to the summit multiple times and for every time they'd scaled it, they'd had to turn back at least three times because of bad weather or avalanche. I gave the Sherpas both of my head torches as a gift at the end of the expedition. I had a head torch for illuminating the outside world, but I had to challenge reality without a torch when it came to seeing my inner world. I had to scale great heights to get to that point.

I took on the Great Wall of China Marathon. It is the third hardest marathon in the world, and I took it on as a non-runner. Talk about challenging reality. I had to pay attention and be in the meditative state to get to Kilimanjaro. When I went to China, which you'll hear about later in the book, I was on a bus. Bus number 7A. Lucky seven. On the bus, I met a wonderful man named Doug White. Doug White was sitting at the front of the bus. I was on the back row, a hangover from childhood, maybe, but I could still pay attention to Doug White. He was a man who'd done many marathons. He'd run 26 marathons across America. When he was on that bus, he was on a marathon roll, doing the Great Wall of China, the Inca Trail, then Kilimanjaro, then he was going to Antarctica, then he was going to the North Pole, all of this consecutively back-to-back. My mind, attuned to challenging reality, was just blown by Doug White. I was adamant that I needed to meet this guy. I needed to know him. This guy needs to become my best friend.

And he did.

He's been a Stevie Kidd Pathway coach and will change your reality at a level that is beyond your comprehension.

Question:

- Who are the people that you hang about with? Who are the people that rise you up to a level that makes you believe that anything is possible?

Let's fast-forward. Stevie and Doug became acquaintances, friends and coaches. Then, I said to him, 'I now know what to do', because now I'm going back to Windsor Castle, which is on my pathway. Once we'd done China, Doug used to coach me every Sunday. Every Sunday, I would get on a call with Doug, and he said he would help me with the five-year plan. It was called 20/20 Vision. Doing some of the hardest marathons in the world.

Once we got to year two, we talked about something that made my hair stand on end. I'm a guy with no hair, and it still made my hair stand on end. Kilimanjaro became a reality for me to do. I'd listened to all of those global back-to-back marathons that Doug had done, and it challenged my reality. All of a sudden, Kilimanjaro was booked up. I was cringing at what I'd done because I'd signed up for

'Kilimanjaro with a difference'. The difference was that I'd decided not to do it in a group, as was the usual way of things, but I'd decided to climb it on my own. I'd have just one guide and a cook. This was quite daunting, because to go and climb Kilimanjaro, you are challenging the reality, by living in the unknown, because I didn't know anything about endurance, I didn't know anything about running. Suddenly, there I was, in Tanzania in a hostel. I'd been coached and my life had been transformed since I met this character, Doug White. I was in a hostel, and I was ready to go alone. Twenty thousand feet, up into the unknown and back down again. You'll be on your own in the camps along the way, the guide and cook will peel off and there's one more thing you're going to do once you get back to base. You're going to run a marathon 36 hours later.

When you take on these endurance challenges and go into the unknown, you realise an essential truth of the Stevie Kidd Pathway. That truth is: Be Coached. The concept of the Stevie Kidd Pathway is not just to coach people but be coached. Coach and be coached, get prepared to ensure you are able to go out and deliver such an event. Through being coached, I'd gone from the guy driving away from coaching the football club manager, to the guy driving a path to the summit of Kilimanjaro. It scared me, it moved me, it destroyed me, but it was there, undeniably there, and it had to be done. I was now a guy with real purpose. My mojo was back. I got to the start lines and finishing lines because of the coaches I'd chosen. I selected my coaches very wisely. Coaches who'd take us to the starting line, hold us accountable, make us relentless, make us turn up for every training session, be on form and in shape to be able to undertake what lay ahead. So, we did. The concept is: coach and be coached.

I had a strategy for the Kilimanjaro and marathon challenge, that I broke it down into small chunks, like a Pac-Man grid, and I focused on the people I was going to meet along the way. By doing this event, the concept of what I believed was possible changed. I discovered who I was and started paying attention internally. That meant I could see more clearly what was going on in the external world.

I was emotional coming off the summit of Kilimanjaro, all the way to the start line of the marathon. It was a release of emotion. Emotion at rediscovering and reinventing myself. That was the power of challenging my own reality and challenging the reality of what people believed was possible. My heart, mind, spirit and intuition was guided by the Stevie Kidd Pathway and that Pathway is here for you, too.

I was back at the hostel, and everybody was celebrating, but I was very quiet, because I was challenging reality. I showered in my room and checked in with how I felt in my body, inside and out. My mind had slowed, and I was finding it hard to talk. I was feeling really accomplished and fulfilled in my achievement.

Word went round the hostel that I was doing the

marathon. A lot of comments went around about me being crazy. I went to my room and tried to talk myself out of it. I considered bandaging my knee. Then a voice came to the side of my head and said, 'Stevie, you'd better shut the fuck up'. 'You're doing this to challenge reality and keep moving forward, searching for what you need to do'.

I was doing it for charity, and it was drawing a lot of attention to me and the Pathway. I was accountable to the charities, and it triggered me out of the negative state I was in. Get a grip, I told myself. You're not doing it for you, you're doing it for them. You're doing it for your family, who are your fuel. Your family, who are in your heart and soul.

All the way round the marathon, I was thinking that I needed to put this into the Stevie Kidd Pathway. Lo and behold, the vision appeared. When I was in a state of gamma, doing the marathon. I saw the event as a consultation. I saw the coaching side of the business. I saw the practise side, the non-exec side. I saw people going on the Reach Your Peak event, I saw Kilimanjaro as part of the Pathway. So, it came to be. Kilimanjaro is now part of the pathway. Is that not an inspirational story?

What's totally crazy about the marathon is that at the start line all of the African runners were looking me up and down... then, we were off, and they were GONE. As I neared the top of the hill at the starting line an African lad jumped out at me from the bushes at the side of and he said that he would run the whole race with me. That's what he did. At the end of the race, I gave him some money and my meal, and I never saw him again. He was like an angel to me. Like a compass I dreamed out of thin air, he simply navigated me all of the way round.

I firmly believe, and it is my right to believe, that he was sent to me.

Are you challenging reality, reinventing yourself and turning it into an actual business model?

From the football manager, to asking myself what I was going to do, to saying to myself that I was going to test my limits, pay attention to my mind, pay attention to the whisper, pay attention to my intuition. Then, I'm going to follow the path, but not interfering, just trusting in the process... all of a sudden, in front of me I can see it! I can see it mapped out like a timeline in front of me. It's shown me the way and the way is:

Consultation, coaching, business strategy, non-exec, brain mapping, Reach Your Peak events, Six Hills in a Day, realign your coaching, your next destination is Reach Your Peak Kilimanjaro. That is the Stevie Kidd Pathway. Going from a man I met on a bus in China, watching in close vicinity the way he undertook events all the way around the world, to then him coaching me and setting out my five-year plan, of which now he is a pinnacle. Doug White.

Doug White, who I'm dedicating this whole chapter to. Meeting that man, him seeing something in me, changed my life. I needed support after that event in China. Doug is now a support as a speaker on Reach Your Peak. He is also a partner in the business for the events side of the Stevie Kidd Pathway for Reach Your Peak Scotland, Reach Your Peak Kilimanjaro and Reach Your Peak Everest Base Camp.

What a story… all because he paid attention to me, and I paid attention to him. Two souls coming together, mirrored, aligned, heading in one direction.

Rediscovery.

Exercise Five

Now... to the Exercise. Remember the moment on the story when I wrote down the top ten things that made me very, very uncomfortable. Running was number one and what did I do? I put the training shoes on, and I ran. Now, what happens on the Stevie Kidd Pathway is that people come onto these events, and they come on and do two years. Then they start to evolve and grow into who they can be. That's when they are finding lots of things that make them uncomfortable. People who do Iron Man, who cannot swim. They have to learn to swim.

What I'm doing now is challenging you. Can you write down the top ten things that make you very uncomfortable. It may be getting a set of drums, it may be learning how to play the guitar, it might be climbing a mountain, or jumping in a lake. I don't know what it is. You need to tell me. You need to tell yourself. I've demonstrated what can happen when you make yourself uncomfortable by walking into the world of the unknown.

Here's your challenge... write down your top ten things that make you uncomfortable, from one to ten. Then, what is it you are committing to do? What is the first step 1? What are you planning to do after that first step? What is it that you are discovering? If you use all of the strategies and techniques that are in chapter three of this book, what are you going to discover? I discovered the Stevie Kidd Pathway.

Who is going to hold you accountable?

I am.

Contact us at <u>inspire@steviekidd.co.uk</u> and share your journey with us. Let us blog about it. Tell us your journey, tell us the ten things that you wrote up. What were the steps that you took, and where did that lead? Did it mean you ended up playing in a band? Did it end up with you doing an Iron Man?

Tell us your story and let's share your magic and wisdom around the world. People can be inspired by this book and this chapter, but also, be inspired by YOU. If you are a complete stranger to me l, who lives on the other side of the world, your story can inspire a person who lives on this side of the world.

Let's start inspiring the world.

Completion of Mount Kilimanjaro and Kilimanjaro Marathon

Stevie Kidd Meeting Doug White for the Very First Time on the Great Wall of China Marathon

Stevie Kidd, Sean Rose, and Ryan Kidd

Stevie During the Great Wall of China Marathon 2015

Stevie Kidd's Daily Stillness Ritual within Nature

Warren Hawke - A Close Friend of Stevie

Stevie with Friends and Role Models

4

THE POWER OF VISUALISATION

This chapter is dedicated to my wife, Lesley. She is a person who has no power over me, and I have no power over her. We have this thing together. We are living in an energy field. We both have aspirations of what we can do in our lives. When nobody has any control over you by telling you what to do and you're living a life of freedom and spirit and what I mean by that is that Lesley doesn't get into my team one and I don't get into Lesley's team one. Then team one and team two, which is as far as we are taking it. Team two then becomes unbelievably strong, because we are watching each other's world and both observing what we are doing and see the world differently. When I come to team two, this is when the magic happens.

Lesley's ability to look at me, say a word, say a sentence, say a paragraph, and, sometimes not even say anything to me, but to just give me this look that basically says, you have the ability to do anything. Even when I fall down. Even when things don't go to plan, she's the only one that's there.

I may be up the nature trail and sitting on my own, then, all of a sudden, team two appears and she's sitting, putting her hand on my leg, her hand on my shoulder, or even just leaning against me and saying, 'you've got this, you've been using the power of visualisation for ten-year chunks, we've just got to go again with another ten-year chunk'.

That is the starting point for this chapter, The Power of Visualisation. It's about having the ability to put it into a big chunk. What does a ten-year chunk represent? Then, the act of bringing it back into smaller chunks. This is where you visualise: 1, 3, 5, 10 years.

Thinking of my own story, my own ten-year chunks and the power of unconditional love... forty years later, I'm still doing what I did four chunks of ten years ago. It's dawn as I dictate this paragraph into my phone, and I'm walking in nature, doing things that other people are not. It doesn't have to be Kilimanjaro every day, just simple nature, whatever you've got outside your front door. A park, a rec, a nature walk. All have the same effect. It's a way to use the power of visualisation. People are sleeping right now. It could be me and Max, my German Shepherd or me on my own, I'm in nature and, guess what, nae body's here. Nature is starting to awaken around me. Birds and insects coming to life. I can feel the air around me, smell it, too. I can even taste the air. I can see more than I've ever seen. Then, as the sky lightens, I start to hear the cars, planes, man-made noises. The whine of the wind and the rustle of the trees, nature.

I sit on a bench, and I start to pay attention to the auditory senses. All of a sudden, it starts to expand, and these dots appear around your head, 360 degrees, and you can start to hear things. As far away as half a mile. As I look away to Ben Lomond, where sometimes I can break the pattern and go away and sit up on a mountain and disassociate myself when the visualisation has become overpowering. I then bring myself back and I train my mind to see more than I've ever seen before. However, there's a secret here… I've been sitting on this bench for twenty years.

As I sit here now, telling you this, I see new things. A house over there, that I've never noticed before, a pylon at the back of the hills, a tall block of flats to my right, that, again, I've never noticed before. They must have been there for a long time. Can you see what I'm trying to say to you yet?

- Unconditional Love.
- Meditation.
- Exercising Your Senses.

Every day, you have to train your senses. See more, hear more, feel more, taste more. If you don't do that, you are going to lose out. It goes back to chapter three; everything is in a brain resonance.

Training the senses.

Do you do that? Do you exercise your senses like going

to the gym? How often do you meditate, how often do you go to stillness, how often do you train your senses by orchestrating them? One at a time and then at the weekend I usually do one per day in the week and then at the weekend orchestrate the whole lot. It's Sunday now, and I've got an orchestra in my head.

Are you getting my drift?

The basis, before we start talking about the power of visualisation is unconditional love. Warren Buffett says that there is no greater power in the world than unconditional love. It's a concept of brain resonance. You'll never access the right side of the brain and blow it up by using the power words of the left-hand side. The example being that from the age of eight, I just studied Mohammed Ali's affirmations, linguistics and then I blew up the pictures in the right-hand side of my brain. Linking back to chapter one, and all of the role models in the left-hand side of my brain. It wasn't my voices, it was all of the role model's voices, blown up in the right-hand side of my brain, with all of the pictures and movies. I'm deep in nature, as I've described, but all I can now see are those multiple pictures and voices of the role models I am summoning up. All I can see are these multiple pictures and movies in front of me that represent those ten years of my life.

That's the emotion state that I live in, all the pictures that I associate to my life wheel and all the pictures that I associate with my business wheel. They are everywhere, it's like watching 500 of them spinning constantly in my head and I can jump into any one of them at any time.

I can *only* do that if I experience unconditional love. Team one and team two meditation. Training and exercising my senses, which puts me in the right resonance. Through using this book, you'll understand how to access the 1% mindset, but you'll need to understand and apply the strategies within the mind that you'll need to do to attain it and access it.

Okay, let's get to work on the Power of Visualisation. You have to ask yourself:

- How big do you think?
- How BIG do you think?

Conditioning your mindset, to the 1%… if you imagine walking through Windsor train station and your non-exec is standing with you and he takes you out of the front door and you exit the station and you look up and the next thing you see, and process is Windsor Castle. Your non-exec says, 'well, that's where you are going to design and deliver a leadership neurology event over three days, okay?' What happens to my mind? Do I get crippled with fear, or do I just let the voices and pictures in my mind take over? I just let the voices and pictures take over, of course I do. You're getting to know Stevie Kidd by now. That's what happens.

How can you possibly, people say to me, have the power of visualisation to see over ten years that every year you are going to climb Kilimanjaro, go to Everest Base Camp? It depends on how big you want the pictures to be. The pictures that you process in your head are linked to one word. Legacy.

• How big do you want your legacy to be?

This links back to role models, because when you set your own voices and pictures and movies for the future, they actually represent every aspect of what you are leaving behind once you slide right into that grave. That's a fact.

In my life, right now, I have my life wheel, with the pictures and voices in that one. My emotional wheel, my business wheel, my development wheel and they are all visual. What have I done in my mindset to condition it? Think about this... with sixty clients, that's sixty life wheels where we've got to visualise and over amplify what lies beyond what my client can see. Then we've got to connect them to what I can see. Not by telling them, but by influencing them. Then we've got sixty wish lists, in terms of what the client wishes for in terms of his life, then we have sixty emotional wheels of where people are living and visualising where they want to live, emotionally. Then, we've got the sixty business wheels which is about visualising where they are now, against where we are going to take them. So, I've not just got the three businesses I'm looking after, I've not just got the ten years of events, Kilimanjaro and Everest Base Camp, what I've got to do and visualise to make that happen, I've now got sixty companies that I've got to do all that for and have all that running in my head at the same time.

- How is that possible?

It's wonderful how powerful meditation is, expressing the power of unconditional love. The power of visualisation comes from when you express yourself from your heart and not your head. That is exactly where my pictures come from. My pictures come from unconditional love because I live my life through my heart. Not my head.

If you love yourself through your head, you don't get pictures, you get analytical data, which is for critics and opinionated types. Hence why I've never stayed there. I gave that up when I was ten. From ten to now I just create the pictures through my heart, and I challenge myself to see beyond how I can think. The more that I do that through the heart, the more they just appear.

The bigger the legacy, the bigger the pictures appear.

The secret to the power of visualisation is practising alpha. Eight to ten resonances in brain frequency in the right side of the brain. Think about a daydream… the more you reduce your heart rate and the more you daydream, I realised this at twelve years old. Daydreaming on my part-time job, my first part-time job, I realised that I had this ability to float into the future and see myself owning my own company. It wasn't just 'daydreaming', I was thinking about what state I was in, I was thinking about what the strategy was. When I became conscious and I was hearing everybody around me, what was going on in my head? Nothing. There were no pictures, no movies, there was no creation. Then, I realised, the children in Peter Pan, when they went into this magical place, a daydream of sorts, and I know I'm recounting the thoughts and feelings of a twelve-year-old, but the frequency of representational systems was evident to me at that age.

I decided that, if I had the ability to shut down the left side of the brain, which meant it turned the volume off, then all of a sudden, I'd let myself create, it was like a picture appearing on the right-hand side of my head. Outside of my head. The more I looked at the picture, the more it was like an artist's drawing or a painting. I could then keep this masterpiece of a canvas, where it would just blow up to the size of something that could have a door in it. I'd open that door and when I opened it, I just jumped inside. When I did that, I escaped reality. Later in life, I discovered it was a state called Epsilon. Epsilon is an out of body experience… jumping into a new world, with new thinking and looking back on yourself.

All of the things that you visually see that I've done in the last forty years has been created in this state of visualisation.

In a state of epsilon, or an arena that I describe as quantum field and quantum jumping. The benefit of accessing the

Epsilon state is purported to be an extraordinary state of consciousness, one of a much higher awareness, and perhaps one of suspended animation.

A Question:
- What is it you have to do now?

What is it you have to do that's going to have people talking about you in hundreds of years to come? Way beyond your life. You'll remember Mohamed Ali, who was able to install powerful pictures into people's minds as to what he was going to do. What's beyond the conditioning of society? What's the mindset that leads to the power of visualisation?

My brother-in-law took his own life. That is now four suicides happening close to me that have an impact on my life across twenty-five years. One morning I woke up with a vision. It was as clear as day. I woke up and I was signposted to make a pitch to do more than that which I was currently doing as an employee of a company. The only way I can describe it is that I was shown the way. At that moment, like the envelope falling off the fridge, I was back at the same place. Visual power, you jump into your own movie. What happens is that you jump into it and then you become it.

It becomes the reality of your future. You enter the state through deep, deep, deep breathing. Then, all of a sudden you are pulled back. As you are pulled back, that's you, back in the room and you think... where did I go there? You know that you were shown the path of what to do next. In that moment, I was called to take action, because the future I'd created in my mind was more powerful than the present moment. It was showing me the way and giving me a man auditory and visual feeling of what life could be like.

What I realised when I connected to this quantum field is that no fear existed, just the power to DO instantly and take action. What I realise when I connect to this quantum field is that no fear exists just power to do instantly and take action.

It's like when you are sitting on a plane at the start of the runway and suddenly, whoosh, the G force hits you.

Read on, read on, but before you do, ask yourself a question:

- Have you ever been given a sign?
- What did you do when you received the sign?
- Did you take action?

or

- Did your internal dialogue or pictures cripple you with fear?

It is ok to be aware of this, but what stopped you looking at the alternative? The alternative it could have been. Look at what happened when it worked out.

There's a saying that children see magic because they look for it everywhere. That's the concept that I've used to condition my mind. I use my mind to see solutions in everything. To never be negative, always be positive... I see solutions everywhere, but I see the magic everywhere, too.

I have a strategy of pictures and movies and videos. I have them constantly about me. They all have some representation to a past success or something that I'm attacking in the future. So, the concept is that I have canvasses everywhere: car, home, in my office, where I have over five hundred canvasses on the walls.

There's the strategy, right there. You need to stop and ask yourself what you do to achieve this... mediation, which I do every day and every night, in all different shapes and forms. Meditation, on the senses, the individual senses, to complete stillness, to daydreaming. Mediation with the pictures all around you, filling your walls.

Where is your life wheel? I spoke about your life wheel in chapter one.

- Is it on your phone?
- Is it on your computers?
- Is it on your fridge?
- Is it on your wall?
- Is it on your car?
- Is it EVERYWHERE?!
- Where are the tools that I am giving you?

You have to have them everywhere and feed your mind constantly.

The power of visualisation rests on the people who are around you that empower you and abet you. The people who get you to rise, making the visuals that you have in your mind go to a level that you can't comprehend. They keep changing, they change in line with your stillness. The more you become still, the higher the level of the visuals.

The more you put your own pictures on the wall, on your computer, on your screensaver, I mean, EVERYWHERE, the better. On top of that, the more you have like-minded people, around you, in your life, all the positive people, who operate at a level beyond you... BANG... appear everywhere.

Peter Pan never grew up. My granddaughter, Sophia, invited me to her imaginary tea party and I went to the tea party and, lo and behold, I hugged her, and I said, 'do you see what I see?' and she said, 'of course, papa, there's water in the kettle, there's tea in the teapot, do you want milk and sugar?' She pointed to the invisible tea cosy, the sugar bowl with no sugar in it, the tea jug with no milk in it and she poured the tea into a cup, imagining that the tea was frothing out. It was pure magic, serious play.

In her world it is real. In my world, it is real, too. The creativity of dressing up into your costume, or being Peter Pan, or Superman, or Spider-Man, but creating this imaginary world, where you take all of the futuristic pictures of who you are going to become. The colouring-in crayons you played with as a kid, that have never been put down by me, Stevie Kidd. What happens to human beings when they stop colouring in? When did YOU stop colouring in? Peter Pan was the boy who never grew up. Sophia said, of course there's tea, papa, and I agreed with her. Her make-believe was as real to her as flying was to Peter Pan. I'm able to believe totally in both of them because I can. Because I choose to believe in magic.

When did you stop colouring in? Never grow up. Always remain a child. That's the strategy. Never grow up. See the magic.

Time to stop and ask yourself something:

- When was the last time you coloured in?
- When was the last time you really, really imagined?
- Are you sitting comfortably because I'm going to tell you a secret? It's a secret just for you, the reader of this book.

People say knowledge is power and that is true. The secret is that imagination is even more powerful than knowledge. Having knowledge, while still continuing to draw, colour in and imagine is very powerful.

The movies and pictures that you associate with, by constantly shutting down the left brain and opening up the right brain by practising alpha every single day, at every single opportunity, you keep adding to the jigsaw pieces within the pictures of the mind that you want to create as a creation. All you do is you go from creating it to jumping right in with the movie, seeing it, immersing in it, with every fibre of your being. It is a strategy I develop people with called Quantum Jumping.

What do you see, hear and feel in the creation of what you hear in your mind?

Second Strategy:

Shutting the curtains off and not paying attention to the past. Even when you are creating that movie of the next five, ten years of yourself, you're shutting yourself down, because you get pulled back. It's like running along a beach with a bungee cord attached to your back. You can't move forwards because you are getting constantly pulled back. What happens is that when you jump into these movies there are some modalities in your head that pull you back into past experience and a sensory language and sensory sequence. You replay something from the past that's an error or a failure, or something that you didn't do well and all of a sudden you have an awareness to shut these down, change the modalities, amplify the future and shrink the past.

It's in *that* moment that the imaginary picture disappears. It becomes small and it just floats away like a shooting star, distorting the past and amplifying the future you want.

The concept is, when it comes to the past, when you shut down a day and it's over. I mean by this that it is over, you SHUT that day DOWN and you never look back. You value that day, and you take the strengths and do an evaluation of what you did well on that day, and you be grateful every day for the gift of life. The gift that you were presented with:

A Day.

You maximised out what was possible for you in the creation of that life, and you then pay no attention to the past. That's what keeps the pictures alive.

Visualise this:

Stevie Kidd's world. Stevie Kidd's world is that he sits in a chair, in a very calm state, all of a sudden about a thousand and one pictures start spiralling around the room. They go round like the solar system within the universe. All of a sudden, all of these frames of reference, all of these pictures and movies that are associated to his life wheel, business wheel and emotional wheel whirl around him.

The question I need to ask you at this point is:

- What are you focusing on 24/7?
- What are your targets?
- What's your focus?
- What is your state?

- What is the power language that you are associating with and fixating on?
- What's your focus on all of these imaginary things that will become a reality?
- What stops you from creating that creation?
- Where does the fuel come from to fuel the ignition for these pictures to appear? What is it that inspires you to create these images?

Imax of Life

When I go to the cinema, I like to go to the IMAX, and I completely immerse myself in the story. It surrounds me, literally and figuratively. That's the way I feel about peoples' stories when I coach them. It all stimulates my mind.

What are the anchors and strategies you have to stimulate your mind to achieve the 1% mindset? Where does that fuel come from?

Mine comes from watching multiple movies, thousands of movies. What does yours come from?

When I think about what the pure essence of the power of visualisation and the most powerful thing, I've done in my life is the KDS Group. I'm working for somebody, but how do I connect other humans with the ideas and concepts that are spinning round my head? What was the initial spark that made me jump through the door and into the movie and take action… Remember? I had to borrow £1700 of my dad. I was ruined, as you'll remember. I borrowed it and kick started the business, if he'd not done that, I'd have found another way, but he did that. When my brother-in-law took his own life, I realised I had to start living. Four suicides later… I'm still grieving. At the time, I woke up the morning after and was grieving and reflected on my own life. Instead of becoming just an observer of your own life, you start to connect to the images and pictures. You then start to see opportunities everywhere. You see the FedEx station, you see the chemist that you've got to walk into, because the images are mirrored in your head, but you've always just been the observer. You have to ENTER.

The concept of entering it and building a seven-figure business, over a ten-year chunk, which transformed people's lives because I built up a multi-divisional business… one guy with a vision, who powers off visualisations in his head, through innovation, who then built this seven-figure business. It was a multi award-winning business from 'lifetime achievement' to 'beyond excellence'. Then would you close it and create another ten-year strategy that meant you started again?

That's the Stevie Kidd Pathway.

The concept of being able to do it again and again, over ten-year chunks. The delivery business was one that I strategically walked away from and then made good with the next business. I had to walk from corporate organisations so that I could run with my next venture, which ran successfully for another ten-year chunk until government funding changed. You have to be able to dance on the moving carpet as an entrepreneur and that is exactly what I've done. More than dance, sometimes I've flown like Peter Pan, up, up and away to Neverland.

Then, I'm ready to go again. The visuals and images this time are about a coaching and consultancy firm. The concept of all of the techniques and strategies that I'd built until that point, led me to create the Stevie Kidd Pathway.

Question:

- What happens when you face challenges? Do the pictures shut down, or do they stay alive?

I've constantly reinvented because I've had the pictures and movies to get up and do it again, better, every five to ten years.

The power of visualisation is mapping out the five- and ten-year strategy of your life and your business.

Exercise Six
Wheel of Life Diagram

Where you Are v Where You Want to Be

Take a visual score, quieten your mind and basically look at every area of your life and if 10 is strong and 1 is poor... where do you think you are today?

Here's a simple tool and graph that you can score in your book with a plain old pencil. Score where you are living today. Then, put the pencil down and just sit back, relax, and visualise who you are. Float to the ten in every area.

Feel

See

Hear

What does ten feel like?

Really feel what it must feel like to actually reach all of these destinations. You are on the Stevie Kidd Pathway, right now. With your pencil down and your mind open. You can feel the psychological shift that happens when you are on the pathway. I need you to realise something. Two things are going to happen:

- One, you are never, ever going to be able to go back. Can you accept that?

- Two, you'll have to accept that what that ten is will get reset to zero.

Think about it. Where you are today against where you are going to be tomorrow. When you have been 1% mindset shifted, the ten you've set becomes zero because YOU have shifted. You've changed. You have so many aspirations for what you want to achieve in life.

Why not go online NOW and submit your life assessment to Stevie Kidd? I'll be more than happy to assist you to ALL of your destinations.

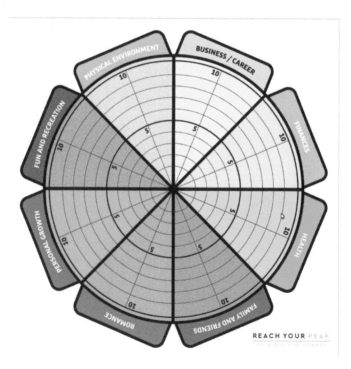

Stevie and Lesley's Wedding Day

Stevie and Lesley During 144 Day Conic Hill Challenge

Stevie's Brother in Law's Grave

Stevie with Granddaughter Sophia

Stevie with Role Model, Muhammed Ali

Everest Marathon at Everest Viewpoint (4000m)

5

MINDSET MASTERY

Mindset Mastery is about... no, don't get comfortable, expecting me to do all the work. You are now almost halfway through the book. Twelve chapters, twelve steps and here you are, at the start of chapter five. You've had my advice, guidance and evidence, evidence because I've given you evidence of how I attained mind mastery.

What have you picked up from the book so far? What have you noted down in your journal and are actually going to copy and use in your life? To try it and see if it has the same impact on you as it has on me, Stevie Kidd. What has had an impact on you? Is it just a book? Is it provoking your thoughts yet?

Where do we start? I've started, I'm sharing the twelve steps and establishing my legacy while I'm at it. Once the book is out in the world, in your hands, it is out there for good. You have Stevie Kidd in your hands and his interpretation of what he filters from the external world? What he filters from his internal world and returns to finding answers to what chapter one was about.

- How are YOU with Day One?
- How do you know you've got what you want?

Powerful questions.

Mind mastery, is knowing who you are and knowing what you want... Let me ask you, because it is the place, we have to start off with in this chapter... how do we follow on from what you just did in the power of visualisation? You were asked to email me, to hold yourself accountable. You were asked to use the wheel of life. You were asked to score where you are. How you see, hear and feel, based on where you are and what your intuition is telling you and where you should be and must be.

Here's the thing in mind mastery... did you play at it? Or did you really embed it with every fibre of your being? A complete immersion of the association to the tenets.

Let me be clear, I'm talking to you from my usual bench I've been sitting at for years, overlooking Ben Lomond. I'm saying to myself that this book is failing to do its job, if it's not forcing you to ask yourself a question:

- Did you do the work?

How many times are you going to read this book? There are

more messages in this book that you'll take up in just one reading. It'll take years to manifest it and understand it and process it.

I'm going to ask you a question. It's a question at the end of chapter four. Chapter One, Understanding Your Mind, Chapter Two, Understanding Your Subconscious, what your beliefs are, Chapter Three, Challenging Your Reality, Chapter Four, Stevie's traits and power in the Power of Visualisation... are you able to say to yourself, I can see myself clearly, hear myself clearly understand in myself, what happens to me when I become a ten? Across the eight areas of my life?

We aren't going to jump to legacy, but we can TALK about the word legacy. That'll be dealt with in the future pages. What I'm saying now, is don't read this chapter unless you've been INSPIRED to reflect, so I'm asking you now, before you read this chapter, five, are you at the absolute 'ten' of where you can be at this point? I MEAN the tens of what is such a wonderful, fulfilled, happy life? Your life on your life wheel. Are you telling me that you're reading chapter five, but you've kidded yourself all the way to chapter four?

- Do you think I'm playing at this?

I'm writing this book for people from all walks of life, across the globe and beyond, for people to pick up these strategies that I have evolved for over forty years and proved, countless times, no matter what happens, that you get the outcomes that you want, when you follow this.

Step One

Pause for ten to fifteen minutes and actually think, have I given this book the credit it deserves? Have I actually got written down from the first four chapters the things that I'm going to do with my life that this guy has delivered to me? I am going to force myself to receive these messages.

Let's scan the book again.

Let's see what I've missed.

THIS is what Mind Mastery is ABOUT.

Ask yourself:

- What have I missed?

What HAVE you missed? Have you missed the eight tens, the areas of your life that are missing the tens? Are you ready for another lightbulb moment?

Are you ready... here it is:

Imagine paying attention to where you are right now. Then, giving yourself permission to go to the tens. Alright? We now know what the eight areas are, we now know what the tens look like, what they feel like, what you see, hear, feel, taste and smell. What happens when you do that and you go on to chapter five, mindset mastery, but you now realise that the tens are always going to go back to a zero. Because, once you chase that hero in you, that future self, that ten it resets. Then, it becomes a zero again.

Think about that for one minute.

We'll now disassociate from that. You are at the cinema, and you are looking at three screens. You look at the first screen and it's how you measure your life right now. Where you are right now. You see where you are right now. Now you look at screen two, which is the screen of the person who has got the tens. That makes you feel amazing. Then, I want you to look at screen three. Screen three is you, evolving and resetting that ten back to a zero. You are setting five- and ten-year chunks. Across all of the areas of your life. THIS is how you attain mind mastery.

The consistency involvement of having the anchor and the metaphor of the hero. This is where you are, here's where you want to be, again how you use language, even though that's not anywhere near where you will be, because that ten is going to become a zero.

I need you to give yourself permission here, to stop, and honestly, honestly, go back and pay attention to where you are today and to the ten and to all the people that inspire you to be beyond the ten. Mind mastery comes from that. Five, ten-year chunks.

Nature Walk with Marley

I'm walking through nature with my dog, Marley, on trails that I have walked in previous generations with other dogs. The dogs that I have had, their natures are with me. I'm now onto my third dog, I'm always smiling and laughing when I'm on the nature trail and Marley sees people walking past and saying, that guy is off his rocker. He sits on a bench and talks to himself, they say. Talks to himself!

- Do I? Am I talking to myself?

I want you to pay more attention to the person you are going to evolve into and that becomes your future self. Who you can mirror, reflect and see? Who are you going to grow into?

- Where are you?
- What's your ten?

Immerse yourself, eighty percent of the time into all of the future selves you are going to be, when the ten gets set back to zero. That's what you are BORN to do.

- Can you BE more?
- Can you DO more?

You know the answer.

The answer is a resounding YES.

Yes, yes, yes.

Say it again. Yes.

The two benches in this picture are the place I undertake mind mastery, by undertaking a walking timeline. A timeline of my life. The point of doing it is that the exercise exists. What does that mean? It means that when I walk round the nature trail, I walk it as if I've been walking it for forty-nine years. If I live to a hundred, I've only got forty-nine years left. Times that by twenty-four hours and work out what to allocate, to dedicate to the areas of my life. How many years am I going to continue to work, or be involved in business? What do I want to achieve in the other areas of my life, because mind mastery is about getting this right? It is about getting every day of your life right. This gives you happiness.

It's taken me 12 years to write this book. I had a real urge to write it when I ran the group of companies. I wasn't happy back then and I wasn't ready. I wasn't happy as an entrepreneur back then, I was doing some amazing things, winning awards for the innovation that I was creating, the business outcomes that I was achieving, but inside no. Where I am in life now, as a wheel, for especially the last 12 years, has been the absolute digital tool that has been in my head like a computer. What I am doing on the timeline when I go around nature is that I go around the timeline forwards, and then I go around the timeline backwards. I walk to meet Stevie at 100 and I walk back to the present and I talk about what I see, feel and hear. I looked through all of the ages of my life and I look in five- and 10-year chunks. I then start to manifest in my head what the targets are going to be. Then, you can imagine, I've got the five hundred pictures floating around my head. I use them. 500 cameras circling my head a bit like the universe. I'm asking you, what do you focus on?

What do you think about? What are your targets? Not focusing on the past, past problems. Mind mastery is about getting these targets and executing them and making sure they SCARE you.

And on the bench, I meet the ten-year Stevies, the Stevie at 60 the Stevie at 70... 80... 90. I talk to them; I believe with every fibre of my being that they exist. I know that everything is going to evolve.

I'm creating Disney movies in my life. Of my life. Of my life to come. Everest Base Camp. Kilimanjaro. Coaching. Chairman. Non-Exec. Business Strategist. Normal coach. Neuroscience coach... all different evolutions. Now there are these strands that all relate to the Scrooge moment. That's what Scrooge told me to do, all those years ago and now I'm doing it. Go to the end, Scrooge said.

My granddaughter, Sophia, is the anchor for me. She gives my life meaning.

Every single day, meditation. Mediation from alpha. It is an absolute must.

You'll remember my huge Velcro curtains that I pull at the end of the day and that's the day done. It's impossible to see back. The hand circling method I use to set the amount of time I want to sleep, you'll remember that.

I'm always up before anybody else. I rise at twelve minutes past four in the morning. When I get up, I put my feet on the ground, my hands on my knees, resting them on top of my legs, I imagine my favourite colours spreading through my body. I do those five times. It takes forty seconds a time. By the time I shower, anything stuck from the day before is totally gone. Down the drain, with the dirty water. Then I look in the mirror and I tell myself that I love who I am. I tell myself that I am going to have an amazing day. I tell myself; I am the greatest. Going back to the role model of Muhammad Ali. The affirmations and linguistics of what they say, internally and externally. Then I go through meditation because I am putting myself into alpha. I go from delta to beta and back to alpha.

I then go into nature and do my meditation. I don't check my phone, don't slurp down a coffee… I go into nature and do my meditation.

My pinnacle moment that is relevant to this chapter is when, at 18 years of age, I collapsed with exhaustion when I was running my first business and ended up in hospital.

An ambulance arrived and took me to hospital and from that moment forwards, I said to myself, I am going to be coached. It was the first commitment I made to myself in my life. Second, was when I was going to understand meditation. Pat Mallon was the master of martial arts that I trained with. One night he threw his red glove up onto the stage. He said to me, Stevie go up onto the stage. Pat had laid down the gauntlet for me. I stood there on the stage looking at the glove and Pat went out to his car. When he returned, he said to me how long did you look at that glove for, Stevie? I said, not very long. Pat said, this is where we start. You have to master your thoughts, Stevie.

At 18 I had a master of martial arts initiating me into the ways of meditation. I built on the length of time that I can hold my focus on the glove.

That was my pinnacle moment for mastering my mind at that young age.

Kenneth Morrison was a trusted friend who inspired me like Doug, as he did multiple iron men events and attended one of my NLP events. It was at this event he installed the world of endurance into me and truly inspired me. I was inspired by Kenny; he's completed 6 iron men and is about to swim channel for 2nd time. If I'd never met this guy, what I am doing right now would not exist.

Lawrie Robertson was one of my pinnacle moments. A role model of mine, someone I admired like a father. A customer of mine but remember... coach and be coached. Lawrie was like a father figure to me. He passed away at the age of 89. He always said to me, let's not talk about age or time and we'll get along fine. We never did.

One time, I went to his house and was invited up to his bedroom where he demonstrated the tai chi that he did every morning. It was his routine that fascinated me. Lawrie then changed into a three-piece suit, he looked pristine, and I assumed we were going out, but, no, he didn't head for the front door. Instead, he went down the stairs and turn left for the kitchen. The message he had for me was that this is how he started his day, every single day of his life. Tai Chi, immaculate, suited and booted even if it was just for a trip to the kitchen, he was ready to take on the day.

That's how Lawrie started his day, and it had a profound effect upon me. How do you start your day?

Like Lawrie, Sir Alex Ferguson was a life role model for me. My mindset changed when he answered a question by saying he was building a legacy. A legacy to build success for the football club that went beyond his life. This had a profound impact on me. I thought, imagine... a legacy beyond your life.

Do you think like this? This book was instigated by that interview. My book will help people even when I'm gone.

A good way to keep mind mastery anchors around you is to look at what you call the people who inspire you, or who are close to you. Here's a question... what do you call them on your phone? Here are a few of mine:

- Jean. The Special Lady
- Sweetheart My Angel
- The Boy Who Inspires Me - Ryano
- Kenny Morrison - The Channel Legacy
- What are yours? Do they need an edit?

Exercise Seven

Put your feet on the ground, your hands on your lap. Close your eyes, relax, do the energy check. Breathe in through your nose, hold it, out through your mouth.

I want to see how long you can quieten your mind for. I want to see when it becomes uncomfortable. The concept of conditioning your mindset to the concept of mastery is that you have to practice conditioning your mindset. You can have yoga teachers, tai chi, martial arts, all of whom will direct you in meditation. Write this down and go through these one, two and three areas and see which works for you.

It might be running, it might be cycling, it might be walking through nature. Find what works for you and email me about it at inspire@steviekidd.com

Tell me how this chapter inspired you and what the noticeable differences are that you will copy into your life.

It's a journey.

Institute of Directors Award

Stevie Kidd with Dough White in London, England, the Day Before Stevie Heads to Nepal and Dough Heads to Greece for the Athens Marathon

Stevie Kidd and his Close Friend Kenneth Morrison

Stevie Kidd with his Best Friend Marley

Stevie Kidd's Tree within Nature for Creating Innovation

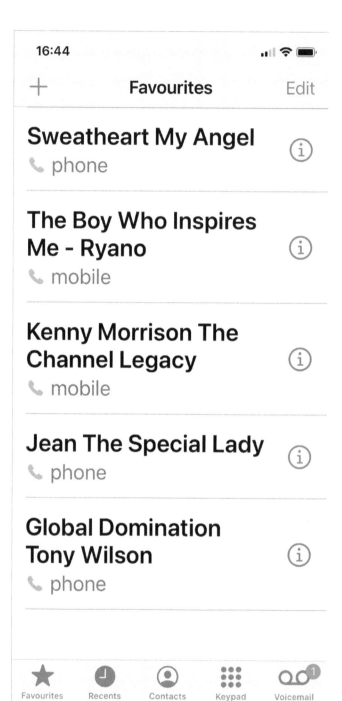

Pattern Interrupt Strategy

6

UNDERSTANDING YOUR PURPOSE

Passion is about vibration and frequency.

Purpose is about what you are SUPPOSED to be doing, not how you are conditioned to be told what you should be doing.

A question to start this chapter:

- What are you doing across every area of your life?

We are not ready to talk about legacy yet, but we are going to allow ourselves to put it on the page. Here it is:

Legacy.

- The vibrations and frequency that you live within every single day, where are they at, emotionally? What vibration and frequency are you on?
- I know what I'm on. What are you on?

- Does it bring you alive?
- Do you feel good for absolutely no reason?
- When you see yourself doing what you were born to do, what state are you in?
- What emotional state are you in?
- What's the feeling of that vibration and are you connecting that solely to the dream because you are living the dream?
- Is that how we can describe your life right now?

Purpose and Passion

Think about what you are doing professionally, but also look at your wheel of life again. I want you to ask yourself a question, based upon where you are and where you are heading:

- Am I living with passion and purpose?

Look at every one of the areas individually. Then look at the emotional wheel. Ask yourself a question:

- Am I living in an emotional state, rather than a negative state? Am I emotionally free?

Emotionally Free

- Am I living with freedom?
- These are the traits; do you have them?
- Am I self-leading?
- Am I assertive?
- Am I a visionary leader?
- Am I leading my own life?

People who live their purpose and passion don't need to be told. They are the people who go out there and make things happen, creating the life they design and desire.

Question:

- Is this me?
- What am I meant to be doing in my life? To be able to see myself doing that, what stops me?
- If you are not doing what you think you should be doing, the thing that brings you alive, what IS stopping you?

Another question:

- If you knew you were going to die one year from today. What would you do and how would you want to be remembered?

- Are you living in the known? How often are you walking in the unknown?

There is a pattern that appears through which you access purpose and passion. That is through having a relationship with somebody. You have to have one amazing relationship. This is taking us back to chapter one here, understanding your mind. For you to truly understand your purpose and passion, you have to know that you are enough. You also need a loving connection with another human being. Once you have both of these, you are away down the path to self-discovery. Once attained, self-discovery leads us to self-leadership. Leading our own lives, enjoying our own company.

Not only is it essential that you can enjoy your own company, but it is also essential that you enjoy stillness and mediation. The purpose and passion that you'll find comes from stillness and listening to the whisper. It's about the daily rituals that you never miss. Every single day starts with that morning meditation. In that moment you see the compass, you hear the voice, and the compass is pointing you in a certain direction. That direction is where you need to go.

You have to give evidence, understand this. Evidence is the one thing that drives people forwards. Where's my evidence, Stevie Kidd, education, but being signposted the way that I'm supposed to live for the next forty years, the next sixty, seventy years. Seeing that way that education was signposting did not fill me with passion or purpose.

Then, all of a sudden, becoming entrepreneurial at the age of twelve, with the multiple jobs and all of the words and pictures appearing, I paid attention to the linguistics, because I realised that the words and pictures that I had in my head were not mine. They had been placed there. Just like they had been placed there by education, telling me what I was supposed to do, telling me what time I had to be somewhere and where I realised very early on that we were all getting programmed, so that the majority of us were going to be walking about in a very deep unconscious state, because we weren't living by purpose. You'll remember the headmaster story from earlier, me interrupting the pattern, seeing purpose and passion across the road. Two lanes appeared, which one would I take?

Join the dots backwards...

I'm now going to ask you a question: I've given you evidence of me finding my purpose and passion, starting my first business at seventeen. What have you done? Reading this book has brought you to this point, where you are meant to be. But are you at the point you are meant to be at? Did YOU bring yourself to this point? Or did somebody else's beliefs or society bring you to this point? Are you filled with vibration and frequency so that when you get up to do what you are going to do, every single day, you are emotionally attached to that? So much so that it sometimes makes you emotional, so that you cry, because of how happy you are, doing what you are doing?

Have society or the beliefs of other people brought you to the point where you are doing what you are doing today?

The second evidence I'll present is a pinnacle moment of my life, when I stood up for my values. You'll find purpose and passion when you live by a set of values. Values that have been installed into you, whether it is your family or your role models. We have conflict in those values when we are not living them.

When I worked for somebody for nine years and I was dismissed because of an incident, to do with driver safety, I was operating from a place of care. This meant that I was dismissed from the company. I didn't mind sacrificing myself for the sake of their safety. I'd be able to start again. When my brother-in-law, also called Stevie, took his own life around that time, that hit me very hard. I was running a super house, and that had become the priority. So much so, that when my brother-in-law reached out for help, I said that I would deal with it in the morning. Then, the morning never comes. The morning never comes, because my brother-in-law takes his own life in the middle of the night.

That was my turning point. An absolute pinnacle moment of the most personal nature. On that morning, when we discovered that Stevie, my brother-in-law, had passed, it was a spiritual shock. So much of a shock, that I shut my auditory down for three months and went deep, deep inside. The question that I kept repeating to myself was, what are you meant to be doing, because it's certainly not working for that company. In that moment, that is when my business was founded, through meditating, listening to the whispers and joining all the dots up in my mind. It was such a vibration, that I had energy that I've never experienced before. I had pictures and movies and voices in my head that I'd never had the like of before then. I was looking at sky-high IMAXs and jumping into them with wild abandon, doing creative things I had never done before. All of a sudden, I had FOUND MY PURPOSE. I'd been signposted by something spiritual; it was like being guided, the four of my friends across my life, who at different stages in my life, had taken own lives, were talking to me saying, Stevie, this is what you were born to do. It's what I empowered myself to believe, it was maybe a way of healing myself.

And I did.

I moved forward and set up my second company. Moving away from employment and doing it on my own. When you start living with purpose and passion you have no idea what you can achieve. Until you achieve it. All of the accolades and awards that came from running that business were built on the back of my purpose and passion. From humble beginnings and a small loan from my dad for that first van, I built it into a multi divisional organisation with a seven-figure turnover.

I was awarded the lifetime achievement award in my

sector; I was awarded the director of the year award by the IOD for innovation youth projects that I had designed. I received an award for youth innovation development and employer of the year. Also, the Highland coalition award for changing people's lives. I received the disaster plan award for corporate organisations and community road safety awards. Customer service awards, beyond excellence and accreditations for Investors in people in business for eight years in a row. These were all a mark of the level of passion and purpose I was living my life with at that point.

I started writing down huge unbelievable goals. I mean huge unbelievable goals because with purpose and passion, if you write down these goals you can believe that anything is possible.

Everybody has to get out of your road because you are coming through. I also had coaches all around me who challenged and supported you to live to your purpose, passion and values.

There is a great life map exercise that you can do. It is where you have to look at yourself at the age of 5, 10, 15, 20, 25, 30, 35... and so on. Above this, you look at the emotional wheel, you look at the life wheel, you look at the professional wheel and the business wheel. You apply a minus ten or a plus ten to see when you were actually LIVING. You join the scores up and it demonstrates a life map of where you have lived in the past to present. You mark off when you had positivity, motivation, confidence, and so on and you see what you are were when you were riding the waves.

The concept of purpose and passion really executes from what you believe is possible. You can start to do a matrix in your head, saying to yourself, if I live to eighty, there are twenty-four hours in a day, how many does that give me? How many hours are left potentially, it's never about existing it's about your life having meaning?

Let me help, living till your eighty years of age, gives you just under one hundred thousand hours of living. When you get up in the morning, and an hour of those hundred thousand ticks away, what is the meaning that you give to your life. What is the meaning you're going to leave as your legacy when you slide into the ground at the very end? Or turned to ash if you prefer to go that way.

If we were all brought through in education system to really discover our values and really discover what our full potential is, by finding a purpose and passion, how would the world be? How would our children be? How would their children be? Is that what scares society? Who knows... all I know is that no matter the successes or failures it was always better to live a life with passion and purpose? Better that, than not living at all.

Think about that. Ask yourself a question right now:

- Am I living? Or are the days just floating by me?

Stevie Kidd lives his life every day, from sunup to sundown. I tell myself every single day that this day is an absolute gift. Every day is presented to me as a gift. I don't know if I'll get up the next morning. Death can strike at random, senseless times, so I'm not going to lose a day, not for anything. I have witnessed much death in my life, so I know how precious each day is to us all.

My understanding of purpose and passion is to BE the difference.

To BE the difference.

To BE the example.

Question:

- How do you fuel the purpose and passion? What is your fuel? For me all my life it is about serving people. I operate from a system of care. I also operate from a system of unconditional love. Caring for others because I can. The years of discipline that I've had of being an example within the community, the country, even the world. The caring aspect within me is deep rooted within my soul. Would you lead a life of serving others, unconditional love and self-leadership? A life of meditating and listening to the whisper. A life of understanding your emotions. If you do, you will find a life of purpose and passion.

The exercise is a question of asking yourself:

- What was I born to do?
- What am I supposed to be doing?

Drop into a very quiet state. Use the image of a running track, perhaps, and ask yourself where you are in these areas of your life. What do you see as the destination of what you are supposed to be doing? Start at the start line, rather than saying where I am and where am I supposed to be and say to yourself: I have arrived. I am here.

Look at the eight-lane running track and see the eight areas of your life. You are looking at those lanes and you accept that, as from today, you make a commitment to yourself, and if that does not fuel you and fill you with desire, nothing will.

Purpose and passion = modelling and mirroring = surrounding yourself with extraordinary people. The more that you surround yourself with extraordinary people, the more you will fuel your soul and find your purpose and passion.

Absolute fact.

Exercise Eight

Sit in a quiet space and look around the room. Look around your world and write down on a piece of paper who the people are that fuel that world. The people who fire up your purpose and passion. Who are the people that do the exact opposite?

Create lists and decide who has to go and who has to stay and who else is still to arrive that will fill your soul with fire. People that will fire you and excite you every day. These are the people that you need in your life. The people that will fill you with confidence and inspire you. You will feed off that.

Having the wrong people around you depletes you. It fills you with embedded negative commands and prevents you from being filled with purpose and passion.

You have to create new thinking to create new realities. That thinking stems a lot from the people that you are around.

Purpose and passion is about awakening the inner self. Bringing what is deep rooted on the inside to the outside. When you do, everything changes. Your aura changes, people will be asking you... what is it about you? You look different and sound different. Best of all is that you will also feel different.

- What stops you from accessing all of this? Do you want me to tell you?
  Yourself.

- How do I do it? How does Stevie Kidd do it?

Once you know you are enough. Once you've got loving connection. Once you've nailed the tens in your life...

Let me ask you another question:

- What is it YOU actually want?
- Where, when and with whom do you actually want it?
- What is it you want REALLY?
- What are the resources you have to accomplish this?
- How will you know when you have it? What will your senses tell you, what will you see, hear, feel and taste when you have it?

What would you look like and sound like? You have to connect to that future state of purpose and passion.

- How will you stand?
- How will you speak?
- Ask yourself, what will happen if you get to this state of living with purpose and passion?

- Going through the eighty years of your life, the hundred thousand hours, what's not going to happen if you fail to get it?
- What is not going to happen if you do not shift?
- What does the rest of your life look like if you just stay where you are?
- How will this affect your life, your family, your business, your job, your friends? What will be the fruit of you discovering your purpose and passion?

I'm asking you. I'm begging you… spend time on this. Do the exercises. Go deep inside. Think of all the people that you admire as role models. Why do you admire them? What are they doing differently from what you are doing? I'm looking at Sir Alex Ferguson and Mohammed Ali on my wall. Lawrie Robertson, an entrepreneur, a father figure to me. I'm looking at all of these people. Then I look at anther wall… Everest, marathon, non-runner, Great Wall of China marathon, non-runner, at top of Kilimanjaro, Kilimanjaro marathon… the list goes on…

Where did I find all of this? I found it by looking within. Quieten the mind and look within to find the answers to purpose and passion.

- What were you born to do?

Stevie and Son Ryan at Reach Your Peak Scotland Event 2

Delegates of Reach Your Peak Scotland 4 (Ben Nevis)

Stevie Kidd supporting the Public Sector on Mindset

Stevie Kidd's Road Safety Initiative

Lifetime Achievement Award for Services to Distribution Sector

Wheel of Life tool within Reach Your Peak Scotland Events

Stevie with Son Ryan on the 100th Consecutive Conic Hill Climb

7

THE ABSOLUTE POWER OF INFLUENCE

The half-way point of the book. A good time to remind ourselves of the rituals that Stevie Kidd surrounds himself with every day. What's the morning ritual that Stevie Kidd does every day? Answer, it is a test.

Yes, he sees all of his future selves and the pictures around his head. He talks about stillness orchestrating his senses and meditation. He does.

I am he and I can't stress this enough. If you don't adopt this way of life, you aren't going to be able to pay attention to understanding yourself, you aren't going to be able to pay attention to the people that are in front of you. The condition of the mind and heart is the secret to being able to influence people. You have to be able to mirror human beings, sometimes multiple human beings, multiple people around the table, at the same time. You have to have your brain operating at a faster speed than everybody around the table. You must, also, have the ability to shut it down, to s-lo-w t-i-m-e down so that you can pay attention to what you are seeing, hearing and feeling of the energy in the room.

Question:
- Have you locked in the previous chapters?
  They were about meditation, orchestrating the senses and creating all of your future selves.

You have to invent the number tens in the business wheel, those which you want to be able to influence people on.

I was always at the end of what I wanted to achieve, so I had to go back and slow my mind, pay attention to the people that I wanted to influence in order to reach the end destination. While I'm influencing, I've also got a picture high on the wall at the top of the room. This picture is of all of the people that I'm influencing. They are in the room, but I have the movie circling the room. The movie is showing the film of the positive outcomes of my influencing.

The above should give you an idea of the things that you'll be hearing about and learning in this chapter. Think of it as a movie trailer for Stevie Kidd - The Power of Influence, the movie.

Right, sitting comfortably... popcorn in hand. We'll start the feature film.

- Who are you and what do you want?
- How do you know that you've got what you want when you've got it?

This takes us back to knowing yourself. Knowing you.

The only way that you can understand how to influence somebody is to understand the way that influence works on you. Mind mastery of your own mind means that you have to turn up every single day. In this mindset, you challenge reality. Do your rituals each day and your mind will be ready to create and innovate.

- Who are the targets? Who are the people that you need to influence? With what I've created in my mind, who are the people that I need to influence?

You need to be in an optimal state. You've trained your brain and you are operating at a faster speed than anybody else. You see things in a different way, and you believe that anything is possible.

The majority of people that you meet, that you are going to be influencing are living in the past as they are present. You are going to be present, too, but you are going to be more future based. You are going to be living in 1, 3, 5, 10-year chunks now.

Enter the room with the people on it that you need to influence, you need to understand that they aren't even going to be close to that. You have to be positive twenty-four seven and see solutions in absolutely everything. You have to smile, get leverage, you have to get rapport and when you are around that table and you are looking at those people, influencing them, it doesn't really matter that you are only meeting them for thirty seconds in an elevator pitch, or you are around that table at a meeting. Being positive twenty-four seven, seeing solutions in everything...

THAT'S the way to BE.

Posture: How do you carry yourself?

You have to stand tall, with your eyes looking straight ahead, with the biggest smile and a firm handshake when you approach people to shake their hand.

Hugs: Plenty of hugs.

Kinaesthetically mirroring and modelling people that care in front of you. Mirroring and modelling as if you were looking in a mirror. That is what you have to do when you are sitting across from or around a table with somebody.

It's YOUR job to excite everybody. To raise people's frequencies and standards to a whole new level. Then, they feed off you. That is how you have to turn up.

You have to be different, be bold and be unique, but above all, you have to be YOU.

Be you.

Remember that the start of this book asked, who are you? Have confidence in answering that question. Especially in the situation of a pitch when you are around that table. You have to awaken, friction, confidence, one mask… you have to be the person around that table that sees the world differently. What you know at every moment. On every occasion do as much of something for the love of it… because you can. When you can demonstrate that, lead them with your heart and with unconditional love in helping others and putting others before yourself, you'll stand out and you will influence people, because they will want to know you.

Understand that it is very easy to influence people, especially when you are living in the 1% mindset of what you will do, against what others won't do. You'll stand out by not living in your comfort zone. You live and walk the path of the unknown unknown. Think of role models or people you look up to. You do so because they behave and act differently. Time to stop observing and start becoming the 1%.

That's like when I went to China to run the Great Wall of China marathon having never run before. As soon as I was in training for the third hardest marathon in the world, people were suddenly calling me and turning up at my office wanting to see me. JUST because of MY actions.

Question:

- What are you doing to call attention to you?

If there are people that you want to influence. There are two ways. You can keep on trying very hard to get a meeting or find a way to carry yourself and live your life in such a way that people are drawn to you. Your energy is coming towards you in abundance. Take power away and create innovation. Pay attention. REAL ATTENTION, to who's in front of you. Every time they are in front of you, demonstrating pain, you are creating innovation. When your mind is still, you are listening to that whisper. You are going to receive that whisper and that idea that they haven't even thought of. This is because, in all of these chapters, up to this point, you know who you are. Now you can pay attention to the patterns of other people.

Model: Model their way with words.

You can pay attention to what preferred representational systems they are using to communicate with you.

Are they using visual language, auditory language, kinaesthetic language? Are they using auditory digital, which is no sensory language whatsoever when they communicate? When you think legacy, a new reality, you are able to think higher, so there's a level of the people that you want to influence and their way of living. It is very important that you don't come across as arrogant in the meeting. You want to be applauding the people in the meeting that are coming up with the ideas and even though you'll get an idea way beyond their way of thinking, you need to influence them by taking them in that journey with you. Even if it means that they think that they came up with the idea.

With the toolkit you are acquiring, you will be able to communicate with anybody in the world at any level.

Another pinnacle moment for me was designing innovation, in response to pain that I had in my life, so that stakeholders who were responsible never experienced that pain. In other words, if I have pain in my life, my brain is automatically trained to become creative and innovative and conjure up a global solution. That's beyond influencing, that is self-leading and leaving a global legacy.

- What do YOU want to be remembered for?

To influence people, you need empathy. That's what I believe. You need to understand the world as you float into people, and you look through those people's eyes and you have to have a perspective of how to influence. I remember sitting in a meeting and sitting quietly and paying attention to every single person in the room, I started to float into everybody and look through everybody's set of eyes. Every time I left one person, I moved to the other. Back round to me was eleven as one - people in the meeting. Eleven all as one person and I could see, hear and feel everybody's point of view.

I'd look to the door and see myself, looking back, that was me, the innovator, and he'd be telling me, this is how to communicate this idea.

I'd stand, put the idea on a flip chart, talk softly, pause, talk to the language of how the majority spoke, e.g., 90% visual representations, I'd draw pictures. If it wasn't, I would stand up on the floor and talk, but I would be repeating the language that I was hearing in the room. I would play that right back at them.

Humour. It is always about the state that people are in. You have to change state. Pay attention to the state people are in when you go to influence them. If they are not in a good state, you have to influence that. Ensure its you with no mask, but you with your confidence, personality, vision and passion, people will see your true values and purpose and be drawn to your energy. Remember, I'm going to embed something that you've locked in in previous chapters:

Life wheel, wheel of life. Emotional wheel, ok you've got this. The person sat in front of you, how do you know that they've not got their life balance? How do you know that they are not happy? How do you know that the way they are feeling inside is not where they want to be? That'll very often be the case and you wouldn't try and influence somebody without paying attention to what state they were in.

I go into a meeting and put the life wheel above somebody's head and start asking questions randomly and innocently, so that I can start to get a picture above their head of who they are, how they are living. Then, I start to pay attention by asking questions about where they should be and all of a sudden, I've discovered just how happy they really are.

You have to be an example across all levels of your life wheel. You have to be demonstrating that you are growing, growing and growing. You have to be different persistently. You have to be the example. You have to be able to never lose touch with society, from understanding a man or a woman who are homeless in the street to understanding a man or a woman who are running a boardroom. Running that company. Stay real to that and you'll be able to operate without making assumptions that you know what is going on in the real world.

Two words are mentioned above, purpose and legacy. To influence big ideas, it means that you are creating solutions. You are creating solutions so that your kids don't have to have the same pain that you had. I did what I did so that my son didn't have to experience the pain that I experienced. I'm going to tell you a story now.

Ready? Well, I'm not quite. To be able to influence people, you first have to be able to influence yourself. You have to pay attention to the linguistics and language you use to describe yourself. You have to have an understanding, back to chapter one again, of who you are, on all levels. Back to chapter one to discover who you are. To have the absolute power to influence somebody, you have to understand how to influence yourself. Do you know who you are? If you are going to be able to understand somebody else, you are going to have to be able to understand YOU.

How do you work out who you want to influence? The people who developed me: Tony Robbins, Dr Richard Bandler, Dr Joe Dispenza, Professor Lipton, Stephen Covey. These are all people that I brought into my life as compasses. When bringing these people into your life, they create different aspirations and movies of what you believe is possible. Then, you look at your immediate family and you want to inspire them, and then look at yourself and think what's possible in terms of potential. That all has an impact on who you are going to influence. What do I mean by that?

Well, I've not been long-term unemployed or been homeless, but I know what that experience is like. I'm not somebody who holds down a job, but I know what that experience is like. When I reach to my potential of running multiple stations, my influence was to inspire my peers. I have them opportunities to be inspired towards that promotion.

Then, we turn to our own aspirations of self-leadership. Perhaps to own your own enterprise. Bear in mind that the people that developed me had been giving me the toolkits, setting the bar as to how far I could actually go. I was aware that my son was looking at me, paying attention to me, because I'd been telling the world that I was going to be setting up my own company.

With that company, who did I have to influence? I had to influence every stakeholder from a 360-degree angle in terms of who you are going to influence. There was one particular group of people that I wanted to influence.

It spoke to the challenge of recruitment, something that people have within the world of business. Here's my formula for the power of influencing people, under one indicator:

- Having no pain within the recruitment strategy, having no people pain within the business, or businesses. What was the power of influence that I had that then created a multi-award winning, multi-divisional, seven figure turnover business?

Here's how I did it: You set up your own business and you have a vision and a concept. I was absolutely clear on my vision and values and my five, ten-year vision. People set up businesses only thinking around today. I set up businesses thinking around the values, visions and divisions that I have for this business.

It started with me, but it wasn't just about me it was about who was supporting me. Now, in 2021, I have my own genius board, who support companies on the pathway by the means of a series of experts on the board who instigate, support, excite with passion to execute that ten-year plan with the customers I have and support today.

In this business, my vision and values were stage one. Stage one of me influencing myself to build on the concept of that vision, value, brand and strategy. They needed to be clearly mapped out so that I could move on to the next stage.

Where did I come from, remember everything is rooted in the nervous system? Why am I, Stevie, coded to be such an obsessive with people? Simple, back to 1990 when I went to the interview for the Glasgow company, I was creating the recruitment strategy for, it was horrendous. From the moment I walked in the gate of the place, horrendous. My recruitment and induction were horrendous. In 1990, there and then, I made a rule for myself that when I set up a company, I would create innovation and a solution that would bring everybody together as part of what I called, a family.

I'm taking you back to experience the pain I experienced, because I'm a pain to pleasure guy. It's a gift to me because it means I can innovate and create a solution.

Fast forward from 1990 to the moment I founded the award-winning seven figure company and we're at the moment of realisation that I can apply leadings from that recruitment and induction pain to my own business.

To fend off the negative learnings of school, including written-by-rote CV's, I asked candidates to come for interview at 09:33 and twelve seconds. Already, I was subverting the process through confusion and hypnosis and then, when they arrived, at the appointed second, I took their CV off them and ripped it up right in front of their face.

Sometimes, I would put it in the bin and set it on fire, for variety. Then I'd ask them to stand against the wall and tell me who they were but forbade them from speaking about academic achievement or work ability. They were frozen to the spot. Imagine experiencing that?!

I was building a business with a family culture, and I needed to be the example. Every day. How I lived my life every day, the standards I set. That's what people saw. Relentlessness with all of these standards every day. It's also about how you are developed and how you are coached and about how you invest in your coaches for senior people. At this time in my life, I was working with the best of six different types of coaches.

Through these rigorous processes a majority of people left, and a minority of people stayed. I spent a lot of time getting to know the people that stayed. What their vision and values were, what was important to them. I hadn't even spoken to them about the strategy and vision. They understood my vision and values and the business strategy, but I was more interested in their human values. Who are they, what did they want to become and what did they think their aspirations were?

They are coming for a job and I'm encouraging them to

think, what am I born to do? I'm that moment there was a kinaesthetic connection. They laughed and said that I had bizarre methods. I said, we have a long-term vision and we're building a family.

We had an employability training company and told these new members of the team that we were all here because we were going to challenge reality. I told them that the world needed a global solution and that I was going to lead it. I needed exceptional people and if I saw that, sitting across the table from me, or standing against the wall, to be more accurate, their CV smoking ashes in the bin, I tell them we are connected and that we're going to create a recruitment culture for seven sectors. I need them to be part of it because we are going to do the same to the people that come on the program. A four-week self-mastery program, all based on 'who am I'. People getting to understand who they were and what their potential was.

We've got eight team members now, ten people in the company in all. Then what did we do? The idea of them just starting a job was ridiculous to me. We rented a house at Balmaha and stayed in it for five days so that we could truly understand one another. Understanding my values, who we all were. Meditation, too, and the mind spa. We then took time on the business strategy and vision, told them who the customers were going to be. The customer was a human being, and we'd take them on a pathway through innovation, strategy and executing the vision.

I used the power of influence and My people stayed with me for 7 years and we had 88% outcomes in employability to a positive destination. It became so successful that we reached seven sectors. All the sectors are raving about us. We are doing videos and the quality of staff is such that people coming through the door are people who know who they are. They were now recruited through normal recruitment channels. We won multiple awards, suddenly politicians in Westminster took notice, the Scottish government took notice, John Swinney, James Purnell, and Steven Timms visited the offices. They basically all asked the same question. How are you doing this? Simple.

We only ask one question: It starts with Stevie Kidd. What did he do differently? He just asked himself who he was and what did he want and how did he know he would have what he wanted.

The answer to that was, because of who he was coaching and who he was coached by who his role models were, that his life had true meaning and he had to lead by example. His example was to create global solutions. That ripple effect went to his family and the people he employed. Then that ripple effect went to his customers and suppliers. Then that ripple effect went to the people he was supporting. It then brought multiple awards, then decision makers came to the business, saying, we've got a global solution here. Stevie Kidd started writing to President Obama and Oprah

Winfrey, influencing them. We were sending case studies and documentaries to 500 people after each academy graduated to people of influence around the world.

Stevie anticipate change coming. Change of direction from the UK government. The whole of the 'Welfare to Work' sector, the sector that Stevie had built a successful business in, changed. Took a different strategy and approach, which Stevie Kidd had already anticipated.

In that moment, he changed direction. Which brings us to the Stevie Kidd Pathway. Stevie was a leader/entrepreneur who executed this strategy and vision.

Question: Do you allow yourself to think as big as having the capability to create a global solution? That was our strategy and that's why we drew the fascinated interest of politicians and also wrote to global leaders. We realised that the impact of the welfare to work forum was a very expensive model for public money. We had a solution that could create a better world. Education kills creativity from the age of five. We built the model, on a nature trail, by the way, and all of a sudden, we were awakening people who were unemployed and had no influence over themselves. We used the burning CV strategy for the unemployed, too.

Exercise Nine

What do you have to do to influence yourself? To believe that you can be somebody that can create something magical that can create a solution around the world that currently doesn't exist.

Write it down:

… and tell me what it is.

We all have the ability within ourselves to achieve anything we want. We all have the same neurology; it's about how we use it. We all walk about with inner stories and inner beliefs that belong to somebody else. That's sad. I was once that schoolboy and it gave me such joy to lead others away from that path and choose the other one.

Build it and they will come… that's the power of influence.

Stevie Kidd's Innovative Employability Strategy and Academies (Multi Award Winning)

John Swinney Scottish Minister Visit the Offices of KDS Group

Multiple Award-Winning Company

KDS Group Creative Room

John Swinney Analysis the Success of KDS Group

Stevie's Stepson Andrew who supported the growth and success of KDS Group

8

OPERATING AT AN OPTIMUM LEVEL

There's a saying I have, and the saying goes like this: *"I've had it and not had it six times."*

There are six pinnacle points in my life where I've had to go back to the beginning and start all over again.

If you can demonstrate all of the rituals and techniques and strategies that I'm sharing in this book, we're up to chapter eight now, nearly two thirds of the way, and if I can share with you the times in my life when I tumbled back down to the lowest point, only to get up, brush myself off and start the climb all over again.

There must be strategies and techniques that I have, allowing me to create the vision in my head and GO again. I'm going to share a story in this chapter, equip you with the techniques and strategies to be able to reflect it back upon yourself, so that, in this chapter, you can find the answers for YOU.

It goes back to chapter one. If you understand your mind

and you understand who you are and you understand your full potential, it doesn't matter what life throws at you. It doesn't matter if life puts you down, you'll always get up.

Put me down six times... ten times, I'll get back up a thousand times.

Ok, back to chapter one, the story with the headmaster. Fast forward to now, the twenty-first-century, two decades in, five forty-one in the morning of a Friday... what'd that version of Stevie Kidd be doing now, if he'd gone and done just what the headmaster told him? He told me to get the fuck back into the classroom, didn't he?! I chose to use my imagination. I saw my twin, over the road, remember, and that twin was guiding me for three, five, ten years into the future. Nobody else told me that I would achieve my goals.

Now, I'm eighteen, unbelievably, it is still the last century, I know, I know, and I ended up in hospital. Why? It was because I'd bought my first business at seventeen. I ended up in hospital with exhaustion because I was working from six in the morning until the very end of the day. Every day. Seven days a week.

Then one day, something just went 'whack', like a knockout punch from Mohamed Ali. Stevie is knocked out. He is only eighteen.

You'll see a diagram at the end of the chapter. This diagram will give you some examples of development that I have undertaken over the years. It will also demonstrate twenty plus coaches, and the non-exec positions that I've had in my life.

What's the message in this diagram? Never stop growing. Never stop being challenged. Pick the right coaches that are going to destroy your beliefs in who you are and potentially keep on pushing you through new doors. When you push through these new doors, you enter new realities.

Doing it on your own, you can get to the end of your life, like the Scrooge story. You reach the end of your life, and you look back and you see that you've not reached anywhere near your potential because you tried to do it all alone.

I'm up to multiple coachees, multiple non-execs, I've spent over £300k on my own personal development, with no fear, just getting it done. Imagine crossing the line of a marathon and how you feel at that point. It's something I've felt multiple times. Hold onto that feeling, because with Stevie Kidd operating on his own strategy, that's how he feels twenty-four seven. Hold onto that kinaesthetic feeling and that picture and that voice in your head. I'm giving you a visual, kinaesthetic and auditory representation of how I feel because I walked away from that headmaster.

Think about it. From the age of five, your creativity and imagination is killed off. How can that be, Stevie? Well, you were born, you become a creative genius, you fall down, you get up, you learn to walk, become more of a creative genius, playing with things, building things, being intuitive, being creative, being investigative... then it changes at the age of five. How is that? It is because you are put into a mainstream school and start to become conditioned as to how you are to live your life. Then, you are led down a path and told what you are going to do for the rest of your life.

Fortunately for me, I never chose that path. It was because I was paying attention at such a young age. I know that I was born for and to do greatness. When you choose this path, you have to turn up every single day. Feet planted firmly on the ground, chest out high, pulled up by the strength of the sun, looking forward to every area of your life that you are going to live to its fullest potential. Would I be doing that right now, would you be doing that right now, without that visual and auditory power?

Or are your shoulders slumped, slanted right over, having weak conversations with yourself... think about it.

Optimal Mindset

Where do we go with it now? I need to take you to a place. Like the ghost of Stevie past. I'm sitting in the steps outside the office of my employability business, and I've locked it up for the very last time. It is all gone.

This is now the sixth time this has happened to me. Has it happened to me, or has it happened to me for a reason? What are the learnings that I have to take from it? A business that was multi-award winning, with a seven-figure turnover, made a huge difference in people's lives, created innovation and challenged reality.

But there I am, on the steps having shut the business. I've got to go up the road and look my family members in the eye and say, 'it's gone'.

Hold onto that thought. What age am I? I'm forty-two. Supposedly, the answer to life, the universe and everything. Ten years ago, from where I am now. At that moment, looking down the road at the business I had founded on that very spot ten years before, I did anticipate what was coming, but I did stand up for what was right by not taking the price.

That's one of the reasons why it came to an end. Building up a legacy in distribution and giving them an opportunity to have everything outsourced with me as the preferred supplier, standing up for what was right, and handing it back across the table, going to their offices and saying, thank you, but it's not for me… I'm giving you it back because that's the price. I know you won't accept the price, but that's the price I'm putting in. It'd be wrong for me to take it at that price. For SO many reasons.

Now, I'm sitting on the steps, and it's all gone. Now I need to RISE again. I need to have some peace. So, when I went up the road, I gave my son a hug and I said to him, give me twenty-four hours, that's all I need. All I needed to clear my mind and wake up the next morning with a new life meaning.

Let it begin.

- What was the first thing I did?

Somebody who is dear to my heart and came into my life for many reasons, and for many reasons he came into Ryan, my son's life, too, is a person called John McKean. He's somebody that I hugely admired in the world of martial arts. He'd already taken Ryan though an eight-year journey to achieving his black belt. I approached John and said to him that I needed his help. I needed his help to train in an art that I'd never trained in before. I asked him if he could do that, and he said, absolutely, Stevie, one on one? When?

Five o'clock, I said. We can't do that, he said, I'm taking classes at that time. No, I mean five o'clock in the morning, not the evening. He gave me one of those looks.

The rest is history. For a long period of time, I picked John up and we went to his academy, and we'd do a routine in calias. We did that for about a year. Sometimes we would train, and I would just say nothing, me, the sticks, the mats and John. One day I hugged him and said, I now know what to do. The message is, operate at an optimal level and hear the whispers. Be signposted and directed in what you have to do. You have to go through a period of quietening the mind.

Just as we were coming to an end, I thanked him, and I left. I haven't seen John since the day I left. I went back to the house and clearly remember passing my wife, Lesley, in the house, she hugged me at the front door. It was seven am in the morning.

"Sweetheart, there's an envelope lying on the computer in the kitchen."

I asked her what it was for. It was a letter from two guys who had come to the home to take it away from us. I looked Lesley dead in the eye and said that I would sort it. I said this with my emotions intact.

At that point. How do you react? You do what Stevie Kidd has always done, from a very young age.

It was in chapter one... the hero twin appears, and he fixates on the one, three, five, ten-year future state. What does he do to create and manifest this creature? Stevie goes to nature, like he's been doing all his life. He walks through and he becomes still, he walks through, and he orchestrates his senses, one at a time and one of the days of the week, he orchestrates them all. He quantum leaps to another universe. He meditates as often as he can, every single day of alpha. Then what he does is he looks at his life wheel, his emotional wheel and his business wheel. He starts to map out where he is because he is back at a starting point again. He starts to bridge all of the gaps in terms of where he is and where he needs to get to by measuring his emotional state every day. Back to measuring it every hour on the hour. Bridging the gaps from where he is in his life, even if his environment is going to change, because they are going to take his house off him. He's bridging the gap tirelessly and seeing where he is, 360 degrees, from above, looking down, but paying attention to the future, to where he is going to go. With that, his feet being pulled to the ground and his head being pulled by the sun to the sky, all he can see is where he is going.

He knows who he is, and he is accepting his identity and accepting where he is TODAY. With every firm belief of every role model that has told him he has a greatness that comes from Muhammad Ali...

He goes again. Moving forward towards bridging the gap. Where that one becomes a ten and that ten will become a one again. That emotional wheel will only be the emotional wheel of the feelings that he wants to attain every single day. To the business wheel, which he doesn't have clarity on yet, but he feels the whisper coming and intuition guiding him in terms of what that business wheel has to be.

I'll now concentrate in what I did going forward, rather than dwelling on the closing of the business. Concentrate, yourselves on the strategies and techniques, going forward.

Time for a question: How would you feel? How would YOU feel at this point? Even if it happened at you one, that you were in the gutter. For it to happen SIX times in your life. How would you feel?

Imagine it, as if you are at the cinema and you are looking

at your life and it's the first time you see yourself, and six times this is happening to you.

- What is it I am doing to get this optimal mindset?

Life Wheel.
Business Wheel.
Emotional Wheel.

They all go back to zero and I need to go again. They are the tools I'm using. The other things I am using are coaches, I look at my life's work, the third of it that I've been training with Dr Bandler, excessively, and at this point I'm revisiting everything that I've ever learned from him. Becoming obsessed, reading and watching his stuff over and over. I'm letting my mind take over my body, spirit and intuition. Consistently quietening my mind and going back to all of the rituals and strategies and techniques that I've given you.

I started to negotiate with some of my coaches, saying I would give some of my toolkit away for free. We started negotiations, there were two coaches that I was paying for and another that had a deal with, whereby I would develop them if they developed me. It was solution minded. Right-brain calming of my mind, not listening to critics, solutioning, even though I was in the gutter. I made a promise to my son that there was no way he was going to see me wallowing in the gutter. I'd seen too many others do it. Give me twenty-four hours, I'd said. My fuel, of unconditional love, of Ryan and my two stepchildren, I wanted them to watch and observe somebody rise again. I looked at my wife, Lesley, with unconditional love and said, watch me. Just watch me. It'll take a couple of years. I'd time lined and accepted that.

What I'm stating is that it's back to the rituals, back to the traits, back to the coaches, back to the tools, back to the development, back to the meditation and we go again.

We go again.

Let's look at the toolkit, the tools that Stevie uses that enable him to be optimal:

Reflect on the place that I was in at that point. Forty-two years of age and a mountain to climb to get to what happens to him in the next ten years. What does optimal mindset mean to Stevie Kidd? Understanding emotions means I can master emotions. Mastering emotions means that I can practise alpha, the most relaxed state of the brain. This allows him to always pay attention and be observant. Every second of his life. He doesn't go onto the negative frequency, that's how he's conditioned his life, his whole life. Never, EVER, have any negative energy around you in your life at all. It's a rule. Stevie sits down in a restaurant, or sits on a platform and detects negative energy, he'll ask to be moved.

You've got to be an example. Never give the past any

of your time. No clutter in your head, whatsoever. You are not here to exist; you are here to take part. See the signs all around you. Through coaching, creating amplifying and quantum jumping, the creative room techniques. Supremely evaluating your life. Sometimes up to six times a day. Absolute speed of execution from that evaluation. Speed of change and incorporated share strategy. The multiple future selves, rigorously, every day, jumping into multiple chairs, the mind spa and the meditative daydream state. Practising theta, practising timeline and future selves, de-cluttering the mind. Doing it through your heart with unconditional love. In nature relentlessly, training hard, martial arts, strength and conditioning, pushing the boundaries. Consistently tell yourself you know nothing, repeat, repeat, repeat all the neurology development. Understand all the states of consciousness, brain resonance, linking mind, body and spirit together. Doing the twinning exercises, remember chapter one, the headmaster and the road, bringing multiple twins into your life. Exercising to a sixth sense. Build and exercise on your intuition. Model, mirror, understand your physiology, the state you are in. Understand the link and power to your thoughts, how you can use language. Language is key. Only accept power language.

Understand the solar system, outside planet earth as your escapism. Your pattern interrupt for what is going on in reality. Understand your brain functions. Who you are?

Understand your legacy. Map it out. Crave caring for others for no reason.

At the point I was having my house taken, I gave all of my gym equipment to a guy who was looking to buy some second-hand stuff and get going. I don't need material things to create my identity. I'm in it for others. No one controls your life. That's a big indicator. Go back to team one again. Work hard at team one, understand what you clearly want. Beyond a ten is always the answer. Stay in high voltage frequency. Define a legacy and be obsessed with it. What's beyond the legacy, what's beyond your life. Understand the programs that you are running.

Quieten the mind at every opportunity. That's crucial to getting to the place you need to get to. Challenge and re-write your story. Learn to let go. Use the power of developing visualisation. Understand what is important to you, what you like, what you love, what you hate and what you are passionate about. Just so you can understand what frequency to maintain on. Don't just exist. Practice influence, pay attention, understand the brain mechanics, understand your family genes and how they worked with coping strategies of reinventing themselves. Challenge yourself daily on how far you can go with outstanding people around you. Bring in the new people, let go of the old. Create a new world. See the magic and positive in everything. Condition your mind and know that that is the way to success and reinvention. Same value culture from working hard with the teams in your life. A hard work ethic.

All of this I did. I am Stevie Kidd. I realised that I had to live to inspire. Be there for others. Be there every day. Be the energy. Pass on to every walk of life this energy. I knew that this would pass and that it wasn't my life. This was something that had to pass. Me, reinventing myself was temporary. I would reap the rewards, I just had to start again. That's what motivates me. That's who I am. My energy, my smiles, my laugh will become more and more each day. I'm going to pass it on and inspire others who will mirror and reflect onto their own lives and say, look what he's doing, things can't be bad. How do you do it, they asked? I told them about my morning ritual, how I look in the mirror every day and I tell myself, I love myself.

Accept ONE frequency. That frequency is the one to embrace life on. Love life each day because each day is a gift. Allow no negativity to come out of your mouth. Let the people around you breathe your purpose, passion and vision. Never stop drawing and dreaming. Always believe in the most powerful emotion know to the human spirit: unconditional love.

That is the secret to creating an optimal mindset.

The big question at this point is: Do you have the discipline to adopt all of these strategies and techniques daily?

I am well aware that from a young age, I had no choice.

I had to find my solutions; I wasn't going to put medication into my mouth to heal me. I had to create my own mindset, so many years of development and neurology have brought me to this point. For decades I've been adopting all of these traits and strategies that you've just read about. I have the discipline to do it every single day. These techniques took me forward. Following on from doing the Windsor Castle event, leaving that event and knowing that it wasn't the future, knowing that doing it once in the biggest castle in the world, watching people leave in a very good state with thought provoking, transformational change, that would take time, because it was all subconscious-based. Now, all of a sudden being deflated and saying that people hadn't turned up at events. There was a voice inside me that said, be patient.

I threw myself into the endurance world. That came into my life by challenging somebody to do something. The endurance world wasn't just about China to Kilimanjaro, marathons every weekend, then half-marathons every weekend, then being coached again. Coaches back in my world and I'm taking about taking the hardest marathon in the world. The Everest marathon.

Everything is moving forward like a steam train and my clientele is building up. All of a sudden, I'm putting it on social media, doing videos, a hundred posts a week. Ryan was turning eighteen and I said to my coach, Casey Morgan, that I needed to do a test as a non-runner, that was going to take on the unknown, unknown, unknown. I needed a test because fear was starting to creep in. That's when the idea of five peaks on one day came in.

I took Ryan for a coffee and asked him if he'd join me on a midnight to midnight five peaks across Scotland for his eighteenth birthday. I wanted to see if I was fit enough for the hardest marathon in the world. So that's what we did.

By peak four, Ben Lomond, I went into a deep state. I could see Ryan's mouth moving but couldn't hear what he was saying because I was in a brain resonance beyond alpha. I looked up to the left and could see Ben Lomond. It was like time had stopped and distorted. It was like I'd floated back to childhood. Floating back in time, like Scrooge. I'm smiling and laughing, feeling a wee bit overwhelmed. A voice was telling me that I was about to meet my destination. I turned to see Ryan standing there. Then I looked up at Ben Lomond and I knew exactly what to do.

Reality kicked in and I could hear noises again. I looked at Ryan and said, son, carry on up the mountain. You go up the top, I'll meet you up there. When I got to the top, I embraced him.

"I now know what to do."

Ryan asked me what was going on.

"Well, son. We've just formed a new business called Reach Your Peak."

We'd risen and we'd reinvented ourselves. All would

be made clear in the future, but we now had the people round about us to create, design and innovate the greatest show in the world. A show called 'Reach Your Peak'. Stevie Kidd coaching. Now once we came back down, I tapped into people like Kenny Morrison, Warren Hawke, Corrine Hutton, Lawrie Robertson, Doug White. I ran it by Doug and he and I supported one another. I used Doug as a bounce board to talk about what we were going to do within this company that I had designed, and it was my whole life in business as an event.

Lo and behold we led and ran our first 'Reach Your Peak' event. With people who were being coached, people at places where I was a non-exec, people that I'd been doing the business strategy for. You had to be coached and assessed for six months to be on Reach Your Peak.

Reach Your Peak One was formed. All of a sudden, we were promoting it in such a way that the world was starting to say, WOW, what has he created in the unknown that doesn't exist in the world today.

Consistently turning up and doing the traits and rituals has proven to be the success in my life story. The company is now called, 'The Stevie Kidd Pathway'. It has a pre-assessment on it. After that you get a bespoke coaching, chairman, non-exec, strategist role: partnership. In that partnership, your journey is mapped out from where you are, to where you want to go. Through that pathway, we then incorporate a product called Brain Mapping. That's where we produce the science and work with James Roy in Costa Rica. With that product, we then introduce brain mapping to give you the science, the SCIENCE, of what lies within you. Once you've gone there, we then incorporate you into an event called, 'Reach Your Peak Scotland', which has nine coaches, nine speakers that are manifested into the design of the event. With those nine speakers we then do six hills, we don't do five, it's six peaks now. When you finish that, you then get your coaching re-aligned. You re-align and start to head towards Kilimanjaro. We pick up the pace again because you've reset everything to zero and we're going again. Now we're heading towards Kilimanjaro with the same bespoke support. Then it's onto a bigger hill. How far can you go?

We bespoke it again and in-between we are brain mapping every four months for you to understand more and understand the results you are achieving. Understand that you are making dramatic changes in your life.

Then, we head towards Everest Base Camp. It all goes back to the starting line of the consultancy stage. At pre-assessment stage, we asked 'how far can you go'? Now that we are about to reach Everest Base Camp, when we get to base camp, we will turn and embrace one another, we will hold one another and we will face in the direction of where it all started and we will take ourselves back to that first stage, where we had the first call, first email, the first text, the first WhatsApp, the one that says, 'can we have a call?'

We will connect that frequency to the frequency at Everest Base Camp. We will turn round, and we will face forward again, and we will look at ourselves and we will say: "How far can you actually go?"

Stevie Kidd.
Legacy.
He has risen again.

He has risen again to pass the baton. A ten-year strategy of handing the baton over to his son.

Ryan Kidd.

The finishing line is:
Here's a message for you and here's an exercise for you.

What are the things that Stevie Kidd really, really embraced to get here?
He never forgot the first time he saw Lesley. He reignited his spirit within to remind himself of how that felt. He never forgot the feeling he had when he proposed to her. He never forgets the day they married. He never forgot the day he first held his son. He made a mantra that day to raise his game as a businessman, as a role model and as a human being. To get the balance of work and family right as an absolute priority. He'd seen too many bad ones to allow that

cycle to repeat itself. He had to be the example.

The concept of a fuel of choice, a fuel of energy, of reminding yourself of your pinnacle moments, when you have that fuel going right through your soul. That reignites the energy to bring about the rebirth.

Stevie kept writing these magic moments down in a journal. Multiplying his neurology, so that when he was in his darkest places, people would be saying to him, why are you like this. They didn't know what was going on within him.

Exercise Ten

If you proposed and married, when your children were born... all of the successes you've had in your life, I want you to write them down. Write down a hundred. Send them to me. Remind yourself and walk through into these one hundred people. All of these hundred magical moments. When you walk into them, you bring the other one with you. They multiply and multiply.

You feel the voices in your head change. You feel the program changing, you feel your physiology changing. While you are moving into those hundred magical, positive moments, look forward and look at all your lanes. See all of your future selves and take that energy and go forward with it.

The exercise is: Can you and have you the energy to beat your mind and find the time and discipline to sit and remind yourself? Get the hanky out, prepare for a good cry.

You are about to discover how great you actually are.

Stevie Kidd with John La Valle

Stevie Kidd with trusted Life and Strength and Conditioning Coach Bernie Hammersley from the EDGE Gym in Glasgow, Scotland (Coach for 15 years)

Stevie Kidd and Ryan Kidd with Casey Morgan (Coach for Everest Marathon 2017

Stevie and Ryan Kidd's Martial Arts Instructor for over 10 years (Ryan reached his Black Belt under Sifu John McKean)

Design Human Engineering Orlando - Dr Bandler

Altered States America and Brighton - Dr Bandler

Charisma Training - Train the Trainer

Life Diploma Coaching Course

Hypnotic Repatterning - Dr Bandler

Personal Enhancement - Dr Bandler (Mind Spa)

Dr Bandler Affect

NLP Practioner Course - Dr Bandler

Advance NLP Practioner Course - Dr Bandler

Master NLP Practioner Course - Dr Bandler

Persuasion Engineering - Dr Bandler

Ascending Your Energy: Tune into Your New Destiny Quantum Jumping (2 years)

Quantum Jumping - Future Self - Design your New You (1 year)

Dr Joe Dispenza : Progressive Workshop

Dr Joe Dispenza : Understanding The Mind

Tony Robbins - Unleash The Power Within

Tony Robbins Creating Ever Lasting Change

Professor Lipton - Your Mind Body & Health

22 Coaches / Non Exec's

Lifetime achievement award (Fed Ex / Brake Charity

Director of the Year Award (IOD) Youth Innovation Development

Employer of the Year Award Social Enterprise

Highland Collation Award Employability and Changing People's Lives

Disaster Planning Award for Corporate Organisations

Community Road Safety Award

British Telecom: Award for Beyond Excellence in Service and Innovation

Customer Service of the Year Award

IIP Each Year Accreditation (Over 8 Years)

Stevie Kidd's Lifetime Development, Accolades and Accreditations to date

Stevie Kidd and Son Ryan Kidd training for Everest Marathon 2017 and creating Reach Your Peak Events

Stevie Kidd with coach Simon Lim after completing Great Wall of China Marathon

Stevie Kidd with close friend Corinne Hutton Founder of Finding Your Feet Charity

9

THE BENEFITS OF BRAIN MAPPING

How do we move on from optimal mindset?
Awareness.

Awareness… I realised my whole life, that I was always in a daydream. I always lived beyond the state of a daydream. Then I recognised a pattern. That pattern was always accepting how things were done, but also having awareness that I was always looking for what was beyond reality. What I became obsessed with was, where am I going in my brain? Where am I going in my mind? Where am I going to create these concepts?

What is it I'm doing across my whole neurology that's different from everybody else, because paying attention to everybody else, caused me to realise that people were playing a lot of noise in their minds? When I was in a daydream, I was always calm. Where does this come from? Does it come from the fast-track paths and the role models and being coached all my life? Does this come from studying seven styles of martial arts? Does this come from spending my whole life training? Where does it come from and what goes on within the mind?

Let me tell you a story, let me tell you a pinnacle moment. It is also to do with paying attention. It is defiantly always to do with listening for the whisper. When I'm in nature, every single experience is different. My mind is still. Three decades of hearing the birds, hearing the cars in the distance, feeling the air across my skin, smelling the seasons of nature, looking at the colours of the trees, looking at the circle of life evolving... who would pay attention to this detail every single day of their life? Who would actually stop and come to a state of delta, sleep, deep unconscious? Who, before they start their day, would want to put themselves back into the daydream again?

It's the logistics of a car with the right foot hard on the pedal. You are in control of all this. I just worked out at a very young age that the mind and the heart are the two parts of the anatomy of the human body that you have to look after.

Two questions: What would your life be like if you found your spot on a bench under a tree, like a mind map? You sat there and just stared into the distance to become still before you'd even started your day, every day and you ended your day this way as well. Who would you be today?

I want you to do something else. I would prefer you to do this in nature. Somewhere quiet with trees around you. I'm quite happy for you to do it wherever you are now, as long as you are sitting down, comfortably, with no noise around you. I want you to do something for me. I want you to place your left hand right over your heart. I want you to put your right hand on the right side of your head.

Close your eyes, softly clear your head and your mind… go to nothing. I want you to focus on your mind, your hand, really focus on the left hand. All of a sudden you are going to start to feel something. That thing you are feeling is called your heart. Pay attention to the beat of your heart and realise that you are now holding on to the two organs that are the most important organs of your life and your human anatomy.

Ask yourself something. When was the last time you connected with these two organs? You'll have an awareness of connecting to these two organs from this day forward. You are going to nurture and take care of them. At the same time, as you quieten your mind and listen to the sounds that surround you, you'll start to hear that whisper, your intuition talking to you. Guiding you.

We now move on to brain resonance. How does it all work? It's time to pay attention and listen like you've never listened before.

Beta - Alpha - Theta - Gamma - Delta

Where the magic lies, understanding the science within, I embrace all areas of the life wheel and link this to states.

Brain mapping for me, is measuring state in emotion in where you live. Emotion controls time, the more you understand and master emotion, the more time you will have and the more in control of your emotions you will be. No matter what the world throws at you, you will not be affected. In fact, you will on average gain 27 hours a day from understanding emotions.

My Development Journey with Brain works – I have been developing myself from a young age, I realised that I could do it with coaches or do it alone. Doing it alone is too painful. My years of development got me to arrive at brain mapping. Working in partnership with brain works allows me to understand the science of what lies within and through undertaking brain mapping frequently I strive to really improve by the guidance of James Roy.

Peak Performance – The brain is like any other organ in the body. If you exercise it, it will perform better. An efficient brain can accomplish more, with greater accuracy, in less time.

Neurofeedback provides high performers with the tools to train and exercise neural nets in the same way as one exercises and builds muscles. The personalised programme makes more efficient use of brain resources by strengthening and maintaining emotional control.

Many high performers have issues related to long term

stress and use neurofeedback simply to promote stress recovery and improve sleep quality: both essential elements to long term brain performance, endurance and resilience.

Professional athletes and musicians use neurofeedback to build the ability to be in the zone: turning out distractions during key situations, increasing processing speed and focusing all their energies on the task in hand. Smoother function equals greater poise under pressure, improved recovery speed after an error, and less over thinking in crucial moments.

This is what distinguishes the best motivation, concentration, and how emotions are handled in high pressure situations. This is why neurofeedback is fast becoming a training standard in many businesses and sports, and increasingly in the business community especially.

Question:

- How much do you want to learn about the brain?

As you will see my brain map graph here, the purpose of this analysis is to compare electro- physiologic activity with standardised age norm data in order to gain clinical insights regarding how the cortex. Now imagine how much your business and personal outcomes would improve for the better if you could control your thoughts and emotions?

By mapping brain function you can find exactly where

"you live" day to day and this can be improved over time. With these insights, we developed a programme to aid the reorganisation of the cortex to resemble age norm conditions. Would you take these traits in return?

What is my advice and awareness to you in the benefits of how you think to how I think, because we all want to know what would be ROI on this way of living and being? Outcomes you will attain – Understand Emotions to master emotions – Practicing Alpha meditation every day on multiple occasions- Start to pay attention – You will hear your inner voice- You will be positive all the time – feeling good for no reason at all – Never have negative energy within you or around you – You will raise your standards and be the example – you will be more present and future thinking – You will have no clutter in your head -you will no longer just exist – be more motivated to learn – you will embrace the unknown – you will execute more speedily - supremely evaluate- more of a visionary leader – change becomes the norm.

Become more aware of your Neurology and your mind will be decluttered – Body – mind – spirit will be aligned – be more open to Neuro Science – pay more attention to your intuition – Become more aware in how you use language – Understand how the brain functions- Understand more in who you are – More aware of your legacy and purpose – Understand you mind – Awareness of your triggers and behaviours – your standards will rise – you will self-lead –

you will rewrite your story – you will heighten your senses daily – Challenge yourself daily in how far you can go – see opportunities everywhere- be more aware of your teams in your life – more aware of the feelings of others – you will simply see magic everywhere – every challenge you see, you will find a solution – you will live your vision – live and breathe your purpose with passion- you will love life - you will recognise every day is a gift – you will be more aware of energy and not tolerate negative energy any more – you will innovate constantly – you will live your life through your heart – you will care more for yourself and others.

Now take a deep breath and pause, as we're going to pause here. Nine chapters in. You'll notice that if you've been doing the exercises, you've been asked to go inside and find some answers.

Here are some questions:

- What can't I have more of what I really want in life?
- What stops me from getting more?
- Am I starting to find out what I actually want?
- Am I finding answers to why I am here?
- Who am I really?

This is the most powerful question and the theme throughout the book. Who are you? Take away that academic ability and the career that you have…

- Who are you?

When you take those two things away and get into the daydream state and gamma, you know what happens… how can you live your dreams, because that is where you see the real pictures and movies that you are to achieve. Are you fulfilled? Are you happy? What's your passion?

- Ask yourself:
- What's my passion?
- What do I believe?
- What of those beliefs need challenging now?
- What's missing?
- That which is in my life right now… is that all there is?
- What's stopping me from moving forward?
- Am I really, really enjoying life?

Don't be afraid. I'll tell you this: the Stevie Kidd Pathway has been designed to help thousands of people across the world. It is just about taking that first step. Before you take that first step… let me tell you a story.

It was a pinnacle moment. I was in America, training with Dr Bandler, a decade ago, training for five weeks in Orlando. One event, in particular was called 'Design Human Engineering', it was training the trainer, personal enhancement, persuasion engineering. It was full on.

There came to a point in the event, in the five weeks, that we explored brain resonance, we explored brain mapping. That's me in the picture, right there, connecting to what was being taught and how I was being developed and then Josie asked me, how do you want to proceed? Time stopped. I just walked away. I finished the course and I walked away; a wee bit confused. Again, the daydream, the gamma state, I was very, very quiet, I heard this whisper, it came right over the back right side of my ear to the front of my eyes, and I see the image of somebody taking to me, I don't know quite who or what that was to this day… it just says… it's not your time.

I walk away.

Hold onto that pinnacle moment and wait to see what follows…

I came back to the UK and started to grow the coaching and consultancy business. I took a path whereby I started offering NLP Practitioner courses. I did that for about a year and then I pulled away. I then started to design and develop my own coaching and consultancy methods, taking me into non-exec, business strategy, neuroscience coaching, life coaching, endurance coaching, and I carried on that path.

Then, all of a sudden, an HR Director appeared, and I coached him for a considerable amount of time, maybe a year. At the end, I remember doing a timeline exercise with him before he left for the last session. I asked him if he could get me access to his CEO? He said, no, that would be impossible. This was because this CEO had multiple coaches in his life. The HR Director went away, and I didn't give it another thought.

I carried on the journey, coaching and developing and gearing up with different types of businesses. I started to get involved in the corporate world and building the Stevie Kidd Coaching and Reach Your Peak brands. The whisper came again… it told me to create a cinematic poster and put it into the David Lloyd clubs, cost was 3k bit extreme but the more I was silent the more I was being pushed forward. So, I put the poster into two clubs, one in Anniesland in Glasgow and one other Glasgow club. It had all of the testimonials at the bottom, like a movie poster.

One day, a gentleman came into the restaurant where I was coaching a client and he placed his business card down on the table and asked if I could see him on Monday. He wanted me to support him. This was a guy who gets things done. A can-do guy. A global CEO who wants to know what's beyond their legacy. We make an agreement and move things forward.

I've got a feeling and intuition inside me, here's a whisper starting to appear… I keep getting the image of the time in America when I walked away… I kept getting the image of the HR director because, this CEO, Jim, has already said, I think you coached my HR director… all of a sudden, the jigsaw pieces are starting to come together. I'm not quite sure how, but all I know is that there is a softness that comes over me that tells me I need to go deep. It tells me that in need to be as still as I can as often as I can, because you know you are going to find the answers, but you need to pay attention.

I fly down to London City and taken to Dover. I'm sitting in Jim's office at his place of work, and Jim stands up and he looks out of the window, towards Calais and then back to me and he says, do you know, I've always wanted to explore brain resonance and brain mapping.

You can imagine what happened to me right in that moment. It was as if my past had just met my present and as I looked up, I could see a clear future.

We had some amazing coaching sessions. When you are working with somebody who is so in tune with themselves, with amazing aspirations for the legacy of their life, it's a different style, it's like being in a bobsleigh. Get in and, woosh, you are gone, with that person. All of a sudden, I got an email in, telling me to go to London. I flew down, met Jim and he said we were going to the clinic. He'd booked me a brain mapping session. The next thing I knew, I was in a room, with a woman in a white coat and I'm getting brain mapped. We have a conversation and go deep into the whole of my life. Then we get the results and Jim and I go for lunch and while he's taking at lunch, I'm not there. I am in a state. A state that takes me to the next stage. When

I came back, the next thing I know, I've got a call arranged with the company that own the brand.

BrainWorks.

I'm then creating and developing that brand myself, bringing it into the business. Now, all of a sudden, I've got brain mapping AND the Stevie Kidd Pathway business. I'm brain mapping clients. Jim, who I work with to this day, is now supporting clients that I support. Jim is now a speaker on the Reach Your Peak event, on brain activity and how the brain works, how to plan accordingly, using toolkits and understanding neurology to plan for the next ten years of your life. In five and ten-year chunks.

All of a sudden it is all coming together. Is that because I am paying attention? I now have a business, Stevie Kidd Pathway, which is at consultation stage and is a bespoke, chairman, non-exec, business strategy coaching stage and then there is brain mapping. Then, it has three Reach Your Peak events: Scotland, Kilimanjaro and Everest Base Camp, where brain mapping is incorporated into the business every four months. For those brain map clients to understand the science of what lies within.

What if I'd never paid attention? Fortunately for me... I did.

Exercise Eleven

It's only fair, having talked about this whisper and a voice that is in a resonance of brain activity when you hear it. Sometimes I hear it in alpha, sometimes in gamma... what I'm showing and demonstrating to you is where I am paying attention and not missing any opportunity. I'm listening to my intuition; I'm listening to my inner voice.

I want you to explore and go deep. Go quiet and be still. Explore an opportunity when a person came into your life, and you missed it. Now that you are on the Stevie Kidd Pathway, you start to become more aware and in tune, in a heightened state all of the time. All of a sudden you have these antennae in your head that are taking in information that you are processing and signposting and saying LOOK!

Write down ten of those moments in your life so far that you have missed. Just like me, and the persistence of never giving up paying attention to the people that come into my life. Can you recall any signs that you missed in your life?

Email me at inspire@steviekidd.co.uk let me know. I am intrigued to know. When you've done the work and done the exercises, you'll be amazed at what you unlock, what you unblock and what you awaken.

Walking the Stevie Kidd Pathway has certainly awoken you to living and leading your life to your full potential.

Stevie Kidd Train the Trainer and Design Human Engineering Event in Florida, USA with Dr Richard Bandler, Co-Founder of NLP

Stevie Kidd understanding Brain Resonance in Florida, USA with Dr Richard Bandler, Co-Founder of NLP

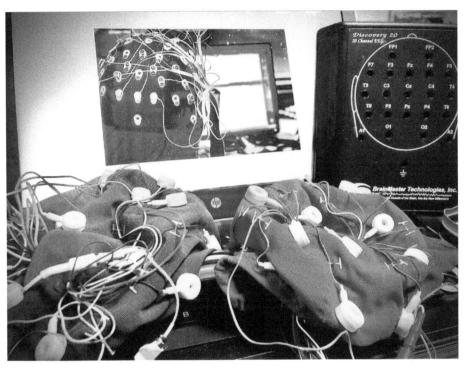

Brain Mapping Technology

Stevie Kidd with James Roy from BrainWorks Neurotherapy partnership with Stevie Kidd Pathway

Stevie Kidd undergoing Brain Mapping in London, England with BrainWorks Neurotherapy

Stevie Kidd with Global CEO Dr Jim Fairbairn OBE in Dover, England

Z Scored FFT Absolute Power

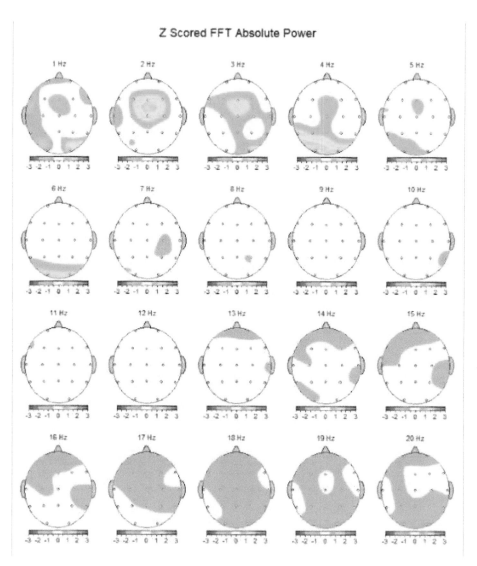

Stevie's Brain Mapping Results demonstrating Stevie's ability to practice a state of Alpha

Stevie Kidd Pathway Logo

10

WHAT IS FEAR?

What is fear for Stevie Kidd? I've never feared failure. What I have been absolutely terrified of, is living a life of regret. If you go back into the previous chapters, you'll see that I've spoken about meditation, stillness, orchestrating your senses… one of the things that I demonstrate daily, is being still.

What I quickly realised is that, when you aren't still, you are either in the past or in the future. You are either in memory or your imagination. You are either remembering or thinking. Either way, both are delusional.

They are not real.
The only thing that exists is the present moment.
In the present, there is no fear.

So, how did I escape fear? It's the same thing that I've been talking about all the way through this book… nature. Being still, because in that moment there is nothing.

There's a stage two to it, also. Being inspired by the people that I surround myself with. I've been fortunate to surround myself with truly inspiring people my whole life. When you surround yourself with people who have done extraordinary things, you mirror them.

Doing that eliminates your own fears. It changes the map of your world, it changes the pictures, it changes the movies, it changes the voices, it changes the feeling, it changes everything chemical. It changes the chemistry of your thinking. This gives you a neurological brain release across the whole of your body. In other words, what I said earlier in this chapter... you escape your own mind.

Mirroring and modelling people who are doing exceptional things allows you to escape your own reality. Escaping your own reality, means there is no fear.

Stop reading. Here's the question:

- How often do you become still?

In that place there is no fear.

Second question:

- Who are you mirroring and modelling?

Who, in the network around you, are you mirroring and modelling? Because if you sit there being observant of those in the other chairs and looking at the people you surround yourself with that truly inspire you... by becoming the observer, in a place of disassociation, you are looking at yourself, but you are also looking at the person that inspires you in your network, it is impossible to have fear.

You are the observer, disassociated from yourself and the person that inspires you. The more you pay attention to the person who truly inspires you, you float into them. Then, you float back into yourself.

You change your blueprint.

You change how you think.

You are escaping your own reality by taking somebody else's reality and constantly involving your blueprint. This means that the pictures inside your mind change. The linguistics and language of what your blueprint map is... changes instantly.

Who is in your life that inspires you and gives you that curiosity, wondering what it is like to be in their life? What is it like to be that person? The more you are curious, drawn towards their world, the less fear exists.

I'll now tell you some pinnacle moments that have come from fear but realigned my blueprint. Realigned my mind map. Realigned the experiences that I've had. In these experiences and the meaning that you give to them... fear is eliminated. This is just my opinion, it's not medically proven. I can only give you my interpretation of my life and my map at the age I am at now.

Here we go, a story. A pinnacle moment.

I remember at the age of thirteen, going inside and saying to my mother... mum, I want to support myself. I want to do this by paying you money, by giving you money, every single week for my keep. What has that to do with fear? I was conditioning my mind for survival mode. Survival of the fittest. How many other thirteen-year-olds would be doing this?

I remember watching a documentary about Richard Branson and in it, he was asked what he put his success down to. Branson's answer: No Fear.

He told a story about being very young and being in the car with his mum. His mum told the driver to stop the car. She then told young Richard to get out of the car and make his own way home. She shut the door and drove away. He attributes this incident as being key to his success and having no fear. How he was conditioned.

I believe that me having no fear at such a young age, going in and saying to my mum, I want to create a survival for myself by paying dig money to her every week, that had a real bearing on my nervous system and coding to survive anything.

I definitely believe that your life experience has a real bearing on the things that make you fearful. All the way from sleeping in the street, to being unemployed, being dismissed from a company, loss of direction, selling a company and not knowing what to do next. Multiple friends taking their own lives. Being lost again. Being financially ruined twice. Taking on contracts and having no fear to scale companies up. Throwing myself at everything with no fear.

Where does that actually come from? I've always been aware, even if you go back to chapter one, that being still consistently and being in a daydream consistently has a real bearing on having no fear. In the moment of stillness, there is no fear.

All there is… is the present.

My stepson Andrew has supported me greatly in building the group. Here's a funny 'no fear' story. Just before the Windsor Castle event, Andrew said to me that I didn't seem excited about the event, you know, at *Windsor Castle*, in two days' time. I was sitting out on the balcony, and I said to him, after a panicked pause, 'I've lost the manual for the event. It's vanished from my computer'

Calm as you like, Andrew takes a seat and says, 'you couldn't rewrite this in the time'. He's right. What Andrew does is extraordinary, he asks me to recite the manual to him and he types it and gets it printed. I am one hour away from delivering event and a bike turns up with the new manuals, just as people are sipping coffee before we start. It is such a beautiful stepdad and stepson story. Andrew helped me to build training company.

Another area here, is how you are developed. I'm going to mention just one man here… Dr Richard Bandler. A man I threw myself into. He goes under the heading of neurolinguistic programming. Tony Robbins is another one. Dr Joe Dispenza… Professor Lipton. All important, however, everything has to come back to Dr Richard Bandler for me.

Understanding all aspects of my neurology and spending fifteen years by this point, teaching and developing myself with everything that this man has to teach. Once you start to become aware of how neurology works and functions… fear eliminates.

It is a bit like lifting the bonnet of a car and when something is not working, you know how to fix it.

Another strategy for eliminating fear is Personal Development.

Being coached and supported to understand more about who you are and what your potential is goes back to the preceding chapters. What was the question?

- Who are you and what do you want?

When you live in the world of certainty or uncertainty. Some people live in a world of uncertainty and the fear cripples them. Some people need certainty in their life. That eliminates fear. Me, as an entrepreneur, I have no fear. The world of uncertainly excites and motivates me. Coaching and being coached is the strategy that I've had my whole life. It is what empowers me to override the feeling of fear. I want to live my life with no regrets.

Question time: When you are on this journey in business and life, and you are doing it alone. How much fear exits?

- How much FEAR exits?

Hold that thought for ten, twenty seconds, clear your mind for the future and ask yourself, how much fear do I have doing it alone?

Look into the future again and see yourself being enrolled in the Stevie Kidd Pathway. You are supported. This is what the pathway stands for. People walking beside you, supporting you… how much fear do you have NOW?

Now float right to the end… Everest Base Camp and you are looking back to consultation stage, two years previously. You see how far you've come. You've seen who you've grown into. Connecting more to who you're growing into eliminates the fear.

One of my pinnacle moments, when I started with Dr Richard Bandler was that he introduced me to a technology called the Mind Spa, a program that I use electronically for different states of trance. He also introduced me to something that made me really stop and think. It was called Senses and Modalities. It was about how our senses give us information in the world and how we code it. It was like putting a remote control in my hand. How we listen, see, feel, taste and smell. The more that we understand that the more that we have an understanding of what is going on. Some modalities are the qualities of our senses, we have more information and richness in certain senses than we have in others.

I was fascinated by it. Then what happened was, when you think of fear, like the remote control, I could press a button and change the visual, auditory, kinaesthetic in terms of how I was viewing things in my mind. I could now start to control my mind in terms of the things that were causing me fear. I asked myself how I could change the modalities of that experience within my mind and how I associated and disassociated to it.

I changed the whole frequency of what was going on in my mind. It is one of the things that I do, and I have been doing for many years: paying attention to people. Paying attention to what I have the power to change within somebody's mind, just by paying attention. The way it works is simply this:

If I can pay attention to understanding every aspect of myself and understanding all of the subjects and experience that I have, then I have the ability to look at others and understand the modalities and sensory experiences that other people have. Then I just need to change the experience by changing the sequence and how it's viewed which means the fear disappears. Instantly.

The question is:

- What is fear?
- Have you ever experienced fear?

Due to my own life experience and business experience, I must admit it was limited. When did I feel the fear?

I felt the fear when I was studying under Dr Richard Bandler, neurolinguistic programming and what I was throwing myself into. How did I overcome it?

Well, it's like a phrase my good friend Doug White uses; the obstacle is the way. You'll either move towards it, or you'll move away from it. I chose to move towards it and straight through it. There is another strategy for what you do while you are going straight through it. You laugh and smile a lot. I mean a LOT. Every single day.

You have to work every day on being 'me'.

You have to lead your life through your heart because that brings no fear.

You have to see the beauty in everything, I mean EVERYTHING. You never feed your fear, when you empower yourself to feel emotion or being caring and sharing, there is no fear.

Can you say the word hero also? Your hero has no fear. You recognise that you can be someone's hero and that your nervous system turns up each day. The more that you can fixate on that one, two, three, four, five-year hero and that becomes the anchor, then you have no fear.

Anything mentionable internally is manageable. Once you've created your own awareness, you can laugh at the utter crap you tell yourself. Pay attention to your thoughts. Initial experience, initial thought, initial internal story created through fear. This is because of your years of conditioning.

I want you to observe yourself and laugh at yourself. These are all strategies and techniques to break down fear. It's not about how much you do. It is about how much love you put into what you do that counts. When you embrace it with love, no fear exists?

Another big one is Not TO Exist. It is all about the meaning you give to life. When you give a big, big meaning to your life in terms of the purpose that you give to it, all fear evaporates. Your mantra is Mother Theresa who said, 'I alone cannot change the world, but I will cast a stone across the water and create many ripples'. It is with you every day, your purpose, what exists is your path, your journey along the path to understanding yourself and the world is absolutely everything. Give your whole heart every day, be kind all the time, don't allow fear to take the absolute joy out of everything.

Self-awareness is the key. Where you live in your head. When you live in your head, you become trapped. Pay attention and care for others. Know who you are. Spend your life on adventures and discovering the world. The world and yourself. It goes back to that obstacle being the way. Connect to it, go round it, go over it, go through it. Stay at the end of the wheel of life, excited that you had multiple different times in your life. What a strategy for overcoming fear. Imagine mapping out six decades of goals.

Quantum jumping is another strategy. As soon as fear kicks in, imagine you are quantum leaping to another world. A world where you are doing it. Twin instantly, perfect quantum jumping. Create the twin next to you. As soon as you feel fear, create the twin. Associate yourself with and float into your twin. Now become the observer. Float back into your twin, the twin who has achieved the goals, remember the earlier chapter with the headmaster? My twin was across the road and that's why there was no fear. Floating into my multiple coaches who are supporting me. Creating a remote control for my head that means I control the modalities, changing them constantly, reversing the psychology, shrinking the fear, amplifying the million dreams, growing more dreams, conditioning my life only to positive thoughts...

Be aware of the power that empowers you to grow by stopping using the words that disempower you. How often do you keep your successes all around you? Everywhere. Immerse yourself in your goals, simply by believing in them. You can do this when you watch a movie that inspires you. This is a simple strategy that is about ceasing watching the movie in your head and paying more attention to the movies on the screen.

Make a difference at every opportunity.

Feel your absolute spirit. You'll be amazed what happens with the power of giving. Living at that frequency, there is no fear. Everything is just learning, and you know nothing. We have no right or wrong, we just have the adventure and the journey to embrace and make everything happen. The journey beats fear hands down. The meaning we give to our life is of a higher purpose, so fear does not exist. It doesn't even get a seat at the table.

Nothing is getting in your way. You pay attention only to using the language internally and externally that brings absolute power. Live in the present. Remember the Scrooge story? That eliminates fear, because it's talking to me and saying you'd better get your arse in gear. How many times have I ever been heard saying that I'm having a bad day? Never.

You ask me, I'll say, world class.

Fear is an indicator of an emotional response. You are creating your legacy with your moving from fear in your life. Bring your force that lies within you. Strip yourself bare to the world, no closet. Set yourself free. What stops you from telling your story?

When you can connect to your story, fear disappears. Communicate it to yourself, carry a journal, replay it and become aware consciously and subconsciously of what you are saying. Don't let your emotions win. Each day you will remain in an emotional state of freedom.

This occurs when you accept who you are across all areas of your life. Being still, mastering emotions, understanding emotions. Do you hear the subliminal messages that you've been getting throughout this book?

Practise stillness today. I've been practising it on every occasion. 6am, who am I, what DO I want Daily. Challenge reality, burn that CV, do not associate with people's critical opinion. Add layers deeper inside you so that your story and belief will stop people's generalisations about your getting to you.

Embrace the fact that you'll be attacking the unknown. The more you walk there the more you will realign your nervous system to give a new meaning to your life. Model and mirror this strategy when you experience fear, stop right away and go and model and mirror. Pay no attention to what anybody thinks. No one walks your journey; fear does not exist in your life. Freedom fulfilled happiness and love. Are you deliriously happy across every area of life? Stay on an anchored frequency. Believe that the world has magic everywhere, even when you suffer fear, it has a meaning for you. Force yourself to identify the magic sitting on the wall in China. The view.

Exercise Twelve

Write down the top three things that create fear for you. I want you to sign up for them.

- Attack them.

- Face them.

- Cut straight through them all.

Contact me at insipire@steviekidd.co.uk and in THAT moment, we will attack that fear. We are taking it head on. Meeting ourselves on the other side.

What are the three things that you are going to commit to, right now, that when you think about them, create fear.

Stevie Kidd in Nepal for Everest Marathon 2017

Stevie Kidd Finishing Line of Great Wall of China 2015

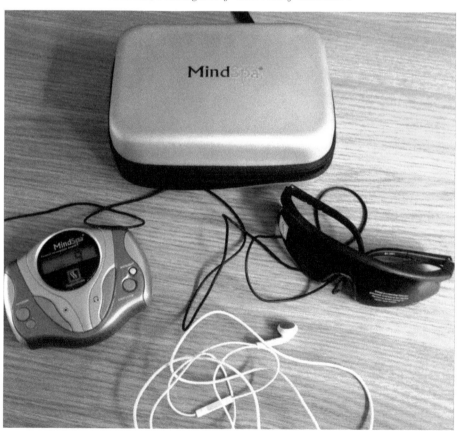

MindSpa

Stevie Kidd Delivered and Designed Self Discovery Leadership Event within the grounds of Windsor Castle, England

The Stevie Kidd Pathway Timeline

Doug White and Stevie Kidd at Glasgow Airport where Doug Delivered and Completed Reach Your Peak Scotland Event

Stevie with Stepson Andrew and Granddaughter Sophia

11

YOUR EMOTIONAL STATE

How do we follow on from brain mapping? How do we follow on from chapter one to ten and take it up to eleven? Chapter eleven is all about your emotional state.

Let me ask you a question. That's right, we are starting off this chapter with a question. It's time to STOP.

- How do you view time?
- Do you ever say that time has run away from you? Do you ever say, where did the day go? Or... this year's flying by.

Here's the question for you:

- Is time an illusion?

Let me answer that before we get right into this chapter on emotional state.

I want you to sit in a chair and visualise another chair in front of you. You are observing yourself in your own life. Pay attention and remember all of the different states that you can go into. There are many. All of the ones that you can remember, can your see yourself in ten different emotional states. Put ten chairs in front of yourself. See all ten of them lined up like a Riverdance line. You are mirroring all those emotional states that you see yourself in. Imagine looking in a mirror. You are looking at ten different reflections of yourself in these emotional states. Look at these emotional states and ask yourself a question. Are you ready?

Here is the question: When you look into the eyes of those individual versions of yourself in those selected emotional states, be it anger, frustration, happiness, boredom... whatever they are, you choose, the question, as you look at every one of them and float into them and then float back, is: how do you view time?

Is time going slow? Is time going fast? Is time standing still? Is time an illusion? How do you answer that question now?

The concept of looking at these chapters and asking, does this guy make sense, because, when you follow these strategies and techniques, paying attention to the stories of my life, you will quickly realise why Stevie Kidd is calm all the time. What does he constantly mediate, orchestrate his senses, use the mind spa... why is that?

What I'm doing is turning the twenty-four hours in

a day into twenty-eight hours. I end up with more time. Understanding emotion means you can master emotion. You need to understand emotion first.

I condition my mind to calm my driver down to a very slow pace, so that I distort time, that means that I've got MORE time.

Read on, because the gift in this chapter is that you will adopt new techniques and strategies that mean you'll have more time in your day, like I do. More time in your month, more time in your quarter, more time in your year, more time in your life, which means that you will get more DONE.

Where did it all start? What is the pinnacle moment? The pinnacle moment was secondary school, believe it or not. I was in secondary school for a month, and I started paying attention to where energy was. I started paying attention, kinaesthetically, to how each classroom gave me a different frequency and vibration. I used to draw wee matchstick men and circle where the feeling was in my body. I wasn't academic and English was the worst of the subjects. Especially when I was told to stand up and read and I couldn't read, or my writing in capital letters, something I still do to this day. I started paying attention to emotions, I even started to pay attention to how time would slow down, dragging, particularly in English. D-R-A-G-G-I-N-G. The hour lesson would feel like a day. Then, I'd notice that when I went to PE, that was an hour lesson that was over in five minutes. I was happy to observe that emotions control time and how time can be distorted. Then, I took it a stage further.

That stage further is the spreadsheet that you'll see at the end of this chapter. It is an exercise that I still do with clients, to this day. Every hour, on the hour, I score my emotion. One to four, five to seven, eight to ten. One to four meant I was calm. Five to seven, ok. Eight to ten was a violent red. I would pay attention to my reds and ask myself, what the triggers to those behaviours were. Then I'd start to discover who I was. Imagine me doing this for years every day. At the same time, I'm meditating. I meditated all through my education.

I then started to do this in my career. Measuring my emotions as I grew businesses. As I ran stations for other companies.

So, here's a question for you: I saw, looking around the classroom, that we are all wired differently. Some people that were good at English classes, would be motivated. I wasn't. I started paying attention to how we all had a different emotional experience of things in the world. I started to realise that we all see the world and the map completely differently. Now we are starting to get awareness to connect to our heart and starting to connect to our mind. We are getting an awareness of where we are living emotionally.

The question is this:

- How do you want to feel every day?

Once you start respecting yourself. Remember the mantra in the morning, the affirmations, looking in the mirror. The cleansing, the inventory check… you have to respect yourself. You have to look in the mirror and say, this is who I am. You are in control of everything within you and everything around you. You are the anchor for how you feel. The power lays in your hands. The question is, how do you want to feel. I'm feeling freedom happiness and fulfilment right now. It's an amazing place to be. To feel that way, you have to feel good about yourself, you have to accept yourself, you have to accept your identity.

It's also about how you talk to yourself and how you communicate with yourself.

Be kind to yourself.

Applaud yourself.

Have confidence in yourself.

Be motivated by yourself.

Stevie Kidd has over five hundred pictures circled around his head. They revolve around his head as he sits in nature, they are all to do with the most lovable moments of his life. The successes of his life, things that make him laugh and smile. From past, present to future.

Coming into nature and spending time in the present, because that is all we have, remember, the concept of connecting to these pictures, of all my successes, all my wins, all my achievements, all of the things that make me feel amazing… that's what I choose to focus on. From the moment I open my eyes, to the moment I close my eyes, the anchor is that I know how I want to feel. Nothing is getting in the way of that. That is freedom. Right there. Waking up in the morning and feeling good for no reason at all. Would you take that? Would you take that right now? Now you know the destination.

What I'm saying, is that if you don't model the rituals, techniques and strategies, that I have, then it will be difficult to understand this chapter. If you don't measure the emotion, if you don't do the life wheel, if you don't reflect from where you came from, to where you are, to where you are heading, if you don't walk the timelines, if you don't become the observer of your own life, if you don't measure the emotion, every hour on the hour, if you don't go and walk every timeline across the eight areas of your life… talking of that one right now. I want you to stop. Stare as if you are looking at the cinema. You can see the circle wheel; you can see the eight areas of your life. There's another soft approach, just looking at how you view life, in terms of how you feel, right now, in terms of how you score yourself, in every area of your life right now.

You can look at the wheel, because there it is, right at the end of the chapter.

How do you feel when you see yourself walking that lane of that timeline? What does that mean to you today? Where you are is where you are meant to be.

What I'm trying to say to you is… what I'm trying to get you to connect to… what is this book demonstrating? What have I done my whole life? No matter what happens to me? No job, no business creates my identity. I'm demonstrating the vibration and frequency that I am functioning from. I have no negative energy; it is all positive. It is all heightened awareness and heightened energy. What am I demonstrating? I am demonstrating that I live in a state of unconditional love and giving and caring. What happens when you go to that state? And what happens when you then start to meditate and practice alpha as often as you can in a day? That means you daydream, you shut down the critical opinion, that you shut down all of the negative voices that are in your head and have been in your head for years. All the beliefs that you have that tell you, you can't do something, you're not good enough. I've managed to shut all that off. In this state, when I'm looking at my life wheel, I don't hear a critical opinion. I just believe, like Peter Pan, flying across the skies, like Scrooge, reaching the end destination of life, I've worked out that this is the state to be in to lead a life of happiness, fulfilment and freedom.

- How often do you give yourself permission to feel good for no reason at all?
- What stops you?

I'm giving you strategies here for you to self-discover.

One of the final messages that I'm going to give you in this book is how I dealt with my emotional state. I dealt with it by not doing it alone. It will be extremely difficult to do what I'm asking you to do if you attempt to do it on your own. There are two things that I do. I have multiple coaches in my life. I tell myself I know nothing. I'm guided by the compass of those coaches. Those coaches have got to inspire me. They've got to be operating at a level beyond me. That's another reason why I stay in a heightened frequency of emotional state.

Here's the other thing I pay attention to. It will lead you into the exercise, which is a fantastic exercise that will take you a lifetime to master... I have the ability to declutter my life, including decluttering people. I remove the people from my life that take me below the line of the frequency I must stay on. I try to influence change, but when I can't I remove them from my life, no matter who it is.

That's because I respect myself for who I am. I will not have that negative energy around me. That doesn't just mean people, that means environment. My office is surrounded by windows, a three sixty view, I won't be put in a box. Car cleanliness is important, too. Sitting in your car, how do you feel? Sitting in your environment, how do you feel. When you sit on a plane... what do you do when you go on holiday? I phone and have conversations with the hotel, with the airline. I tell them who I am and where I want to be positioned on that plane and what room I want at the hotel. I'm controlling all of those factors by reaching out and communicating. It is future thinking. All of the things in the future that can put me into that state.

Think about it; when you book a holiday, do you just go on holiday and randomly wait and see where they put you? Or do you book a holiday and start communicating with everybody, believing that you can have the ultimate experience of feeling amazing. That's what I've done my whole life.

Where's the motivation factor in that? I value how I feel. That's the anchor. I want to feel like that every single day.

The fuel of choice, where does it come from for Stevie Kidd? It comes from unconditional love. The unconditional love I have for myself, my wife Lesley, my son Ryan and my immediate family. They are my life. For everything to make sense that I've covered in this chapter... you know what my fuel of choice is... my immediate family.

- What's your fuel of choice?
- What fuels your soul and makes you unbreakable?

Exercise Thirteen

So, the exercise is, have a look at the spreadsheet, from the moment that you wake up in the morning, on the hour, every hour, right in a number. Do this for a week. Then, colour code them: red, amber, green.

- Green is one to four.

- Amber is five to seven.

- Red is eight to ten.

If you want support, contact Stevie Kidd at inspire@ steviekidd.co.uk. I will happily turn that whole chart into a green. See if you can do this for a week. See if you can do this for a month. See if you can do this for a year. See if you can do this for the rest of your LIFE.

Start to pay attention to the reds. Contact somebody like me to help you get all of those reds to green. Get to self-discover why you have all of these behaviours and triggers that engage patterns that lead to negative states.

Next, I want you to look at your way of life. Look at your way of life and where all of the negative energy is. What are the things that you've brought into your life that bring you into that state? A state that you don't want to tolerate any more. What is it that you are no longer going to tolerate?

What are the new things that you are going to bring into your life that will bring a new emotional state of freedom and feeling good for no reason at all?

- Start to make a list.
- Start to create an awareness.
- Get the two minds communicating with one another, so you can start to create a self-awareness.
- Start to take action.

This will mean that you start to communicate with people at hotels. It will mean to phone ahead to restaurants, telling them where you want to sit, because you are now realising what puts you in that state.

The most difficult thing to do, is making a list of the people that you can no longer tolerate in your life because they put you into that negative state.

Who are the people that you are going to being into your life that will empower you to remain in that state?

Stevie Kidd at Innovation Centre Offices of Stevie Kidd Pathway

Stevie's Collage of 144 Days Climbing Conic Hill Consecutively

Stevie Kidd peers who also completed Great Wall of China Marathon meet again to Complete World Dopey Challenge with Disneyland Orlando, Florida, USA (4 Races in 4 Days)

Stevie and Lesley Happy Place, Villamoura, Portugal

Daily Schedule

Week: ######   Start Time: 7:00 AM

▼	Mo ▼	Tue ▼	We ▼	Th ▼	Fr ▼	Sa ▼	Su ▼
7:00 AM							
7:30 AM							
8:00 AM							
8:30 AM							
9:00 AM							
9:30 AM							
10:00 AM							
10:30 AM							
11:00 AM							
11:30 AM							
12:00 PM							
12:30 PM							
1:00 PM							
1:30 PM							
2:00pm							
2:30pm							
3:00pm							
3:30 PM							
4:30 PM							
5:00 PM							
5:30 PM							
6:00 PM							
6:30 PM							
7:00 PM							

Measuring Emotions (How Much Do You Really Want To Know)

12

HOW TO BE ENTREPRENEURIAL

So, you've arrived. You've arrived at the last chapter. I want you to ask yourself something: How do you think this is going to go?

Do you think it is going to be all about me, Stevie Kidd? Obviously, I'm going to have to start the book and give you the seed.

- Where did it start?

Meditation is about becoming a flower. You need to do all of the groundwork before it can blossom and become a flower. People want the flower, but they don't want to do the work.

How can I start chapter twelve in a way that gives you the fundamental meaning that Stevie Kidd has been entrepreneurial all his life?

Part One

There was a factory and it closed down. Eight thousand people lost their jobs. I watched this eight thousand people at a very young age, SOME not recovering, SOME not understanding, their blueprint being their nervous system, their life map being every area of their life. All of a sudden, their life had been distorted. They didn't know how to recover. That was all they knew.

I reflected this back on myself and said, what are you going to do with your life? How are you going to build yourself up, so that, no matter what life throws at you, you will always stand tall, with the sun pulling you up to the sky and the ground sucking your feet down INTO THE GROUND. I was thinking like this at a very young age.

That was a pinnacle point in my life. That's the moment I made the decision at a very young age, still in single figures, Stevie Kidd the kid, that I was going to be entrepreneurial.

- I was going to be different.
- I was going to be bold.
- I was going to be me.

Where does the fuel come from that allows me to become entrepreneurial and Peter Pan, to be innovative, to be creative. Look at the Pathway. The Pathway is innovative, there is nothing like it in the world. Look at how I did distribution, look at how I did employability, look at how I did youth programs.

Whatever base metal I touched, I turned IT to gold. This, said by the senior executive of a corporate bank.

- Where does the FUEL come from?
- Unconditional love.
- Giving.
- Caring.

What was the chapter before this? Emotional state. Where does Stevie live? I've reflected and asked you how you've lived. I've given you an exercise to find out where you live. I've given you an exercise that gets you to the frequency of vibration.

- Why do I want you to get there?

I want you to find your greatness. I want you to stand tall and realise how great you actually are. To get there you have to have this feeling of being inspired by yourself and your own life story every single day. So, where does Stevie's fuel come from? His son.

I'm looking at a picture of me holding Ryan at the age of three months and remember making a commitment to him that he would be my best friend for the whole of my life. I'd be taking that role on as team one, looking after me, team two, my wife, being a husband, team three, being a father. That's my fuel of choice.

What is it that gets me into that state to be entrepreneurial? Taking those three roles very, very seriously.

Let's stop the chapter for a moment.

Imagine there are three chairs on one side of you and three chairs on the other. I want you to sit in chair one and look across at the opposite chair.

You are looking at yourself. I want to ask about unconditional love. How much love have you got for yourself?

Move your chair two and look across at the other chair two opposite you. You are now going to look AT that person you met for that first time, proposed to, married and then had a child with. Go inside yourself and feel how much unconditional love you have for that person.

Then, go to chair three and do the same. Look across at your son or daughter. Think about the moment that you heard your wife was pregnant and the heart connection you felt at that moment. Remember the first time you held your child in your arms and the great promises you made, telling them you are going to do great things with your life, and you were going to inspire them so much. Do you feel it?

Stand up, go across to the other side and sit on chair one and float inside yourself to view the original person. Look from that person's eyes and feel what they feel. You are now seeing through that person's eyes, looking at you with empathy and really giving unconditional love as you are now feeling the other person.

Move to chair two on the other side and move into somebody else. You are now going to float into your wife or your husband. You are going to look through the eyes of your wife or your husband and you are going to look across to yourself and see just how much unconditional love they receive from you. What are you feeling right now, do you have conflict, could you do more? Is it a different feeling from what you believed when you were on the other side?

Hold that and ask yourself:

- Could I do more and be more in that relationship?

Go to the next chair and do the same for your son or daughter. Look back. What do they hear, see and feel of you? Feel free to do it with your other children if you have more than one. If you are being honest with yourself, you will have just found out a lot about yourself, especially through floating into your family and looking through their eyes.

My fuel of choice comes from empathy. I won't make assumptions on my head as to what I believe. I look through the eyes of the relationship I have with myself and the relationships I have as a husband and a father. By jumping onto their souls and seeing things through their eyes, I'm getting clarification. When I touch my heart and look through them, I will find my answers.

I invest every single day, in those relationships, because they bring me the fuel of unconditional love, happiness and belief that I can do anything.

I know how many times I fell. They have always been there to lift me back up. All I have to do is commit every single day, to invest in those relationships. That is the commitment I have. That's where that fuel comes from. It's my fuel of choice.

Now that you have your fuel, now you understand, you need to understand something else. Where is it that this comes from. How is it this animal created that delivers consistency every single day? Uncomfortable.

Every day has to be uncomfortable. What demotivates me is living in comfort. You have to make yourself uncomfortable. Constantly tell yourself that you know nothing. Constantly develop and learn every single day. I mean learn every day. Even if it is something that you have done before, read it again. You will interpret it a different way.

The message here is uncomfortable.

Part Two

Legacy.

You need to create and change the lens in your eyes. You need to put in the lens of all of your role models. All your coaches. The people that you admire. You need to slide the lens over your eyes, and you need to look through their eyes. That's the eyes that you choose to look through.

Then, what you need to do is put something that you stare at right in front of you. It is six letters.

L-E-G-A-C-Y

You deserve to have a life of meaning. You have to contribute. You have to believe in your greatness. You have to *believe* that the things you can't imagine that the things you need to give yourself permission to imagine the things that you don't believe you can imagine.

Remember the Windsor Castle event? Coming out of the train station, me, looking across the road at the biggest castle in the world. Thinking, one, you'll design an event, two, you'll deliver it in that castle.

In that moment, meditative, calm. A controlled emotional state, chapter eleven, Stevie boy delivers!

You need to believe, but don't look through your own set of eyes. Looking through just your own set of eyes, you limit what you believe is possible.

Now that we've changed your eyes, we now need to change your auditory internal. We need to replace and start paying attention to all of the words and voices in our head and even how we pitch. We need to stand tall; we need to look with this new set of eyes, we need to say, I've just posted it. The picture of me with a thirty-kilo dumbbell on my shoulder, looking straight ahead and saying: I am amazing.

This is what you have to do. You have to believe in your ability to tell yourself every day and pay attention to the language that calls POWER.

POWER

This is what I need from you, I need power.

I need for you to go in and think about yourself every day in this one percent marginal gain. One percent improvement every single day across every area of your life. Going into a daydream and seeing yourself achieve beyond a ten, where are you now? Where are you going to be? Does the ten walks to you? Walk to your ten-standing tall. Heading straight towards it, coming straight through. Believing in yourself, you are going to get to that ten. All of a sudden it becomes a zero. It becomes a reset, because you never catch your hero, you never catch your destination. You've got multiple destinations, plans for five years, ten years, fifteen years, twenty years. This is about how you talk to yourself, internally, but also adding the voices of your role models, orchestrating them in your head, while you look forward and say to yourself that which you truly see yourself doing.

Give yourself permission. What do you truly believe that you were born to do? The concept of me coaching clients and the Stevie Kidd Pathway is, I see more in you than you see in yourself.

I want you to stop right now and ask yourself a question. With a quiet mind and with all of these wee traits that I've put in this chapter, get yourself into this state.

Now you ask yourself:

- What was I born to do?

  See yourself.

  Hear yourself.

  Feel yourself.

- *What was I born to do?*

Give yourself permission to float into that space. Float into that space and imagine you have two chairs in front of you. Or alongside one another. One is who you are today. You have the other one that you float onto when you sit in that other chair, you become that person. You have become that world. Then jump into a third chair and just fixate on the observer. Observing oneself that is achieving that goal.

Put your hand on your heart. Feel your heart. Look at yourself. Think how amazing that would be. How proud of yourself will you be? Seeing yourself achieve and do something. If you can manifest this in your mind, you can bring this to a reality.

I truly believe in you.

I truly believe that you can go inside and become great. In every way.

In every day, in every way, you can become better and better. Every single day. If you don't believe it, you install my voice in your head. You start listening to the voice I am giving you because you were born for greatness. You can exceed the potential of how you see today. Just by changing your potential. Imagine picking up the remote control of a telly. You turn it on, and you are in control of the dials. You are about to orchestrate, to create that 360-degree IMAX of your life all round about you. As you soon round, you see yourself living the life that you deserve. In all of the lanes, everything is a ten. You keep walking up through the lanes and you meet yourself as a ten. Next lane, meet yourself as a ten. You keep accumulating all of these tens and you stand up tall with the ground sucking you to the ground and the sun pulling you to the air. With that feeling right in your soul, you look ahead, and you see the end. You see the end with a smile on your face… because you are fucking amazing.

Every time you look in the mirror in the morning, you just see me sitting there on your right-hand shoulder, smiling and saying…

I believe in you because I know how really amazing you real are. Now go and make it happen.

What is it I'm asking you to do, now that you've got all that greatness, you have all that belief? I need you to self-lead. I need you to operate ahead of your timeline. I need you to be assertive. I need you to be dynamic. I need you to lead. I need you to be a visionary leader. We all have it within us. You just need to look into your life and see when you had these attributes and then look at your role models and check how they do it and model them.

I need you to look after yourself. I need you to take care of yourself.

- Spiritually.
- Nutritionally.
- From a health point of view.

You need to care for yourself. You need to respect yourself and you need to applaud yourself every single day. You're not here to be a survivor, you are here to be a creator.

All of the chapters in this book contain the attributes that you need to become an entrepreneurial, visionary leader.

I'm going to ask you a question:

- How many times did I fall down?
- What happens when Stevie Kidd falls down?
- He gets back up.
- What happens when Stevie Kidd falls down again?
- What motivates him to get back up again?

He started from nothing, just him as a human being and he went again. Fast forward to where we are now. Writing this book that you hold in your hands. Creator of the Stevie Kidd Pathway.

When I look at the Stevie Kidd Pathway, one of the things I'm really proud of, is that it's not there to rebuild human beings. That pathway is there to change generations. When I work with people on the Stevie Kidd Pathway on how far they can go, what happens is that all of their friends, family and children all change life direction, because they are truly inspired.

My life's purpose is your children's children. Bringing forth a new form of innovative leaders, entrepreneurs. On the Stevie Kidd Pathway, we support people to have this mindset in life. We say there is a ripple effect. Forward generations, all generations to come.

- Are you giving your best every day?
  I mean, your BEST.
  You have it in you.
  To give your best.
  Every.
  Single.
  Day.

Use this book as your toolkit for you to acquire the life you desire and the life you want. I have never overslept! I have never had a day off! I never say I will go for a wee lie down! I never go to see doctors! I am just truly blessed and excited to get things done and be the best I can be every single day.

Exercise Fourteen

Now that the book is completed. Browse www.Steviekidd. com browse and see how you can change your life. You'll see a pathway. A process. That process is in the consultation stage. What am I looking for out of the consultation stage to make sure that person is in peak state, ready to get started? What's the strategy and technique that I have that I can pass on to you? For you to incorporate this strategy into your life. To put you into that peak state so that you will be ready to return to me. Reach out and convince me that you are coachable. That you are ready to take that next step that you could potentially take to the grave not having achieved.

Here we go, it is called the genius board. The genius room. How does it work? It is a strategy I've always had. I've never had board boardrooms; I've always had genius rooms. Are they board or bored rooms? I'm not going to ask people to commit to a board room to be creative and talk about the future, am I?

At the end of my day, before I go to sleep, I do one more ritual. I go into this imaginary creative room, called the genius room. There are six monitors around the room and eight chairs in there, too. I put the people in there that I truly admire. The people that take me to another level, even when I mention their name. The monitors show captured points of my day. My most motivational part of my day. An area where I need to improve. Your intuition will tell you what I mean. In a daydream state, I listen to feedback from Sir Alex Ferguson, Mohammed Ali, Kenny Morrison, my mum, my son, my wife… all the role models that I have in my life. They are telling me about my day. I don't speak. I simply acknowledge what I think I am hearing from them. I go round and each of them gives me a message to take into the next day. They also tell me what they think of me. They give me a compliment. Compliments are something that human beings don't like. I get compliments every night. From the eight individuals in that room who appear to me. I take those messages into the next day to improve in every single way.

The question is for you:

- What is your genius board?
- Have you got the discipline and strategy to undertake a visual technique like this?

Go into your creative room and evaluate your day. Your role models, because you admire them, they know what to say. Listen to your whisper and listen to your intuition. They will all give you messages every single day which improve you as a human being in life.

You ARE on this planet to make a difference.

To care.

To give.

To contribute.

To make the world a better place.

That is what this book is all about.

For you to go inside and acquire the tools.

For you to be the difference and make the difference. Every single day.

Love to you all.

I am Stevie Kidd.

Stevie with Parents Andrew and Sandra and Ryan with Grandparents

Stevie Looking over the Great Wall of China Capturing a magical Moment

Dr Richard Bandler Co-Founder of NLP Delivers at Week 12 of The Stevie Kidd Online Masterclass, helping support many people all over the world during Global Pandemic

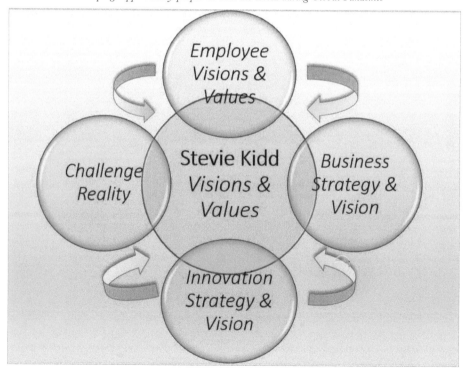

Stevie's Entrepreneurial Formal to Success Model

Stevie with his Sherpa Thile from Nepal who supporting him at Everest marathon 2017

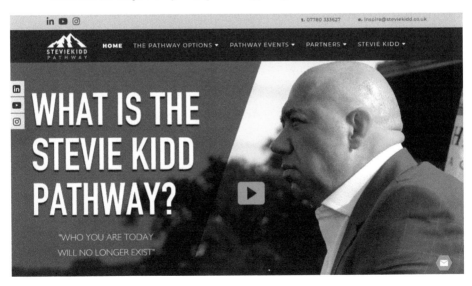

Stevie Kidd Pathway Website (www.steviekidd.com)

Stevie with Wife Lesley on their Wedding Day

EPILOGUE

There is nothing greater for the human soul than caring for yourself and discovering yourself, because once you do that, there is no greater force out there than being able to touch another human being.

You have to understand yourself before you can take care of others. The more you understand yourself, the more you can give to others.

SK

Then and Now - Stevie and his son Ryan

Lightning Source UK Ltd.
Milton Keynes UK
UKHW020231020822
406680UK00006B/356